"Captures the energy of Hawaiian waves – and surf culture – through smiling Irish eyes!"

Mark Cunningham, North Shore lifeguard and bodysurfing supremo

Sunset at Three's:

An Irish Surfer in Hawaii

Sunset at Threes: an Irish Surfer in Hawaii

First published in 2024, under the imprint of The Manuscript Publisher

ISBN: 978-1-911442-50-9

A CIP catalogue record for this book is available from the National Library

Typesetting, page design and layout, cover design by DocumentsandManuscripts.com

Cover artwork by Elizabeth Cope

Charitable Contributions:

Beyond production costs, proceeds from this book will be donated to the Surfrider Foundation and the Bureh Beach Surf Club, Sierra Leone

Dedication

To Shandy and the Surfers – Mahalo……

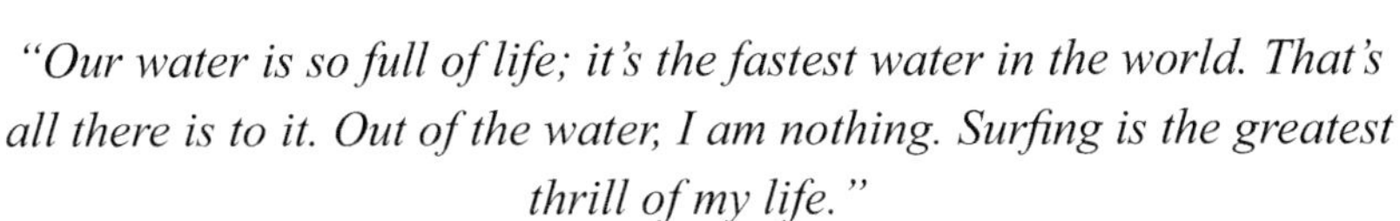

"Our water is so full of life; it's the fastest water in the world. That's all there is to it. Out of the water, I am nothing. Surfing is the greatest thrill of my life."

"I always eat whatever I feel like eating. I eat fruit, vegetables, steak – anything. I eat pie and ice cream if I want it."

"Don't talk – keep it in your heart."

Duke Kahanamoku, "The Big Kahuna" and father of modern surfing

Contents

Preface

Hawaii and Ireland, Ireland and Hawaii – Ireland plus Hawaii, maybe, or even divided by it. That was the equation, the challenge, I guess: for a surfer, and a superficial one, on the surface, it seemed so easy: warm water, blue skies, famous waves – versus the quiet, subtle, earth tones of lesser-known waves in the cold. This is, pretty much, the story of that divide: just a story – just some tales – of the way the waves break, and the way life goes, in each place.

And here, pretty much, is how it played out: because Hawaii, cool as it, isn't the place you necessarily plan to end up. And, even if you do, it isn't, maybe, the easiest pace to get to: way out there in the ocean, and not too many Irish people, and sort of small. But San Francisco, where I had had some glory days, had not worked out so well in the end– if you were not pushing the tech envelope, you were just licking the stamps – and so the big, big, bad, beautiful move back to Ireland was on the cards – the move home for ever, after a long time away.

Then – as happens some times in life – a few things happened: Covid arrived, and I got a call about a job in Hawaii, and I had to wait a year to get all my clearances, and, well, in the end: what are you going to do? Wait out the Covid storm at home, and then light out when the vaccines arrive? Go check out Honolulu, just for a change of scene? Go find out whether, as they say, Hawaii can be curative – go and see if all the answers are down there, out in the Pacific Ocean?

And so, for three years – from, like, 2021 to 2024, give or take – I ended up living that life: in Honolulu, work across the road, and one of the best waves on the island – a place, for whatever reason, known as Threes, or Three's, or other versions of the word – down the street. I had the boards, got to know the locals, tunes in to the local energy, and stayed as fit and healthy as I could, and lived for the surf. Technique improved, and surreal waves were ridden, and there were mind blowing moments – but there were also injuries, alterations, drama, comedy, and the constant question: was there really any contest between the topical aquamarine and the North Atlantic gun metal grey?

As it turns out, there was: as it turned out, there was a lot more to Hawaii, and to Ireland (where I retreated for the winter) than met the eye. Unexpected twists, precarious turns: tropical superficialities giving way to realities, and the booming, bombing winter swells of the Irish west coast putting Honolulu into a different kind of perspective.

And this is how it sort of played out: the stories of the arrival of a newcomer to Hawaii, but also the story of how someone even gets there: leaving other places; waiting out pandemics; all the time edging closer to the turtles and the sunsets – and that whole scene. Even after getting there, there were trips home, and stark contrasts, and back and forths, and contrasts, and change in direction – and back again, to floating in the dusk in the Hawaiian ocean.

Maybe it is a tale of globalisation, or the pandemic, or just of surfing: maybe it was a phase of life; or a transition, or an evolution, or the end of an era, or the start of an era, or maybe the whole thing was something else completely. Maybe, though, it was actually nothing much: just some moments from the surf, home and away, that I reckoned needed to get written down before they got washed way – like pretty much everything to do with surfing always does, for better or for worse.

But, yeah – maybe, as well, there is a little more to it: maybe there is something else that comes out of the mosaic, but I am not totally sure what it is. The waves broke, the tide changed, the sun set and the moon rose – and it happened all over again, again and again: yet somewhere in between the rhythms of the ocean some parts stood out, and stuck, and carried their own stories with them, all on their own – and here they are.

Foreword by the 'Father of Irish Surfing', Kevin Cavey

I for sure cannot take credit for what follows in this book – though Sebastian, or Bassie as he is better known, often says to me that I was the reason for it. Not because, he says, I brought surfing to Ireland – but because once I brought, in a small way, Ireland to Hawaii.

That adventure began many years ago back in the sixties, when both Ireland and Hawaii were very different places. They were, actually, breathtakingly different – with Hawaii taking the laurels in so many respects, but Ireland also paying to its strengths. As a young, born-and-raised Irish surfer arriving in Honolulu for the first time, I am pretty sure that I was the first of that hardy breed in the islands.

At twenty-one years of age, while working for my father in the family-run hotel in Ireland, I was dispatched to USA. When I got to the West Coast, I made a bee line for the beach and borrowed a board and got in to ride my first Californian wave. But, I thought, there has to be more: I felt a sudden urge to go the extra mile. The picture of Hawaiian surfers and hula girls jumped to mind – I might never be here again, who knows! So, I went for it: a travel agent on Market Street issued my round trip to Honolulu flight tickets.

Sweeping in over Oahu was a delight with the town, the beach and the sparkling ocean filled with surfers. The airport was a very large version of Dublin Airport: inside it was a buzz of activity with troops in olive green or suntan beige uniforms, all most likely going to Vietnam. I rented a mustang conversable and drove down the coconut palm lined road to the city, and then to Waikiki and directly to the YMCA, where I dumped my bags grabbed my board shorts and went to the beach. The bay was magnificent, with its attractive apartments at Diamond Head on the left and the Pink Lady hotel and the Royal Hawaiian on the right. Behind the beach, the land had not been built up – the area was still filled with coconut palms and banana trees. I rented a twelve-foot tanker and plunged into the turquoise water: as I paddled out, I met gentle swell which got larger as I went. Now at about two hundred yards from shore I met my first proper waves – could I have been at Three's?

Anyway – wherever I was – gradually I moved closer to the curl, where the tough crew were taking off. Soon afterwards, I took an enormous wipeout that pinned me to the bottom after spinning me round and round. In those days there weren't any leashes so one had to paddle after their boards, and that is what I had to do while all the time feeling desperate. After being run over by the remainder of the set I managed to get things together!

Next to surfing I had other priorities, like Pearl Harbour. I zoomed that direction: en route I saw a Marine thumbing a ride, and I pulled over. Lieutenant Jiménez, who was clad in suntan shorts and Marine shirt bounded into the car. He was grateful for the lift, and was going to the harbour as well. It was a great experience. Jiménez then invited me to go bowling and after that to his house for tacos and to meet his Mexican wife. What a kind fellow – I hope he did not go to Vietnam.

Those kind of experiences were so rare those days: today, in the modern global village, we have all been brought closer together. Likewise, no doubt there are eternal differences between Ireland and Hawaii – the weather, for one, though even climate change might change that! – but there are also more and more commonalities. Ireland has become a surf destination; Hawaii is no longer a remote place but on where the work truly meets on a daily basis.

Over the course of my life I have often reflected on the questions that are asked here – which is better? In what way? Does it matter – can you get the best of both? Can an Irishman ever truly thrive so far from home?

Here are the answers! In a raucous, reflective, comical series of stories, Bassie takes us back and forth from the green waves of

Ireland to the aquamarine ones of Hawaii. You will be shocked, amused, possibly repelled – but it is all true, and it is all real. I know, because I have lived it myself. Wishing my good friend – who has (for now, anyway) chosen the Island for his home – all the best. May the force be with you, Slan, and Pomaikai i ia' oe – enjoy the ride! Mahalo,

Kevin Cavey

November 2023

Prologue: Do It for Ireland

On that first, big crowed, intense, overwhelming day – who knows, August 16th, 17th, 18th? – it was hard to get myself over the ledge. Hard to believe it was happening: the majesty of the waves, the North Shore cohort – the famous faces, the locals, the sun, the everything. Ethereal, magical, intimidating, and intense: the usual option, even at home, would have been to hang back a bit. On the road, especially in Hawaii, such a feeling was doubled: leave it to the locals, mate, and pick up some scraps.

Because, I can promise you, nothing can prepare you – and nothing, nothing, nothing can prepare you if you have come from the Irish Covid winter – for what you see as you paddle out: the sun, the waves. The colours, the crowd – the undulation of each surfer – each uncle, wahine, brah, auntie, as the sets roll underneath them, and lifts them up to the sky: the dance, the weaving, the thousand suns mirrored off the aquamarine ocean, past the snow-white foam and in to the cartoon-blue sky; the colours of boards and boars shorts an bikinis popping out at you everywhere; the impossible lines drawn on the wave. it is, truthfully, sensory overload – more than the mind can process.

Just one small thing, though: you really, really need to know what you are doing. Because, for one reason or another, I guess if you stay out long enough a wave is going to come your way, and one did for me. And, just then – looking at the Irish colours and the Hawaiian colours, on my board – and though neo-nationalism had been exposed for the nonsense it was in recent years – and though I had been reading about historical figures who mistakenly backed the nationalism vibe, and ended up causing world wars – I felt, at that moment, that doing it for someone, or something, bigger than myself was necessary.

And so I paddled, and the wave jacked, and I looked down on the crowd from what felt like a long, long way up, and the decision point arrived – and I paddled some more, and I thought of one of the lads from home, who had said, "Yeah, sometimes, for sure, you need to get your scrap on" – scrap being Irish vernacular for squaring up to situations – and I thought of the Irish football manager who had said "You have to put them under pressure": and I said to myself, via an inner voice – not out loud, fortunately – I said to myself, "Do it for Ireland".

Do it for the country that shaped you; do it because I was the only one out there from that neck of the woods. Do it because they knew I was Irish, and they knew that Ireland had waves, and I wanted to represent. Do it for Ireland, and do it for Hawaii, and do it because I wanted the wave – do it to create a moment that would be documented and remembered, I reckoned – at least inside my head, if nowhere else – as I flew down the face.

Hawaii 1: At the Showers

At the showers: Where it all began.

At the Showers

Things had progressed, for sure, since I got off the plane, though not by much: I had started work but was still waiting for my boards; I was unsure about Hawaii, but still going for it. I was still in a hotel, but had found a place to stay; I was feeling better – but still a long, long way off the level of *bien-être* of just a month before.

Anyway: there was no way of knowing how it was going to unfold, basically, but the surfer at the showers, it seemed like, might have some leads. He was there most evenings, and didn't look too approachable – but then no surfer ever does, really, particularly after surfing: always abstracted, or surrounded, or exhausted, or just somehow adrift. But, who cared: one evening, walking by, I asked him, as I had asked a few others, about waves – and how, in particular, he could surf a shortboard on the south shore. Wasn't it only for longboards down here?

So we got to talking, and he let me know where to paddle out, and when to go, and told me that the wave was amazing, truly amazing – and Zachary seemed cool: wiry, fiery, highly strung, highly educated and a former rock and roller, with his piercing blue eyes and surfer-length hair he had a vague Don Johnson look that covered a super yogi nature: a black boardshorts man, I noticed, and a vibe that held strong opinions on pretty much every subject on earth.

Half listening to him as I took all this in, it vaguely felt like a foothold: I was just about to move into a surf shack up the road, and it seemed like getting the closest wave to me dialled in was going to be the priority: as always, laziness and convenience would probably make the rules. Little did I know that that one wave was also going to be the best.

Spartan Living

If you want to surf in Hawaii, keep it local – right? I mean, don't go traveling around to all the other breaks and start from the bottom each time – am I right? "Find the right wave, and then live and love beside it": that might, possibly and briefly, have been a sort of 70's Hawaiian surf philosophy that went out, probably, when all the surfers got cars.

The idea was, also, not to put down roots: Hawaii was meant to be a light touch, unlike San Francisco: a last staging point, before Ireland. I had learned the hard way in SF that your prized possessions were just other people's junk, and Hawaii was pretty much reductionist anyway: a place where less was more, where needs were few, and where you often just needed some clothes and flip flops and avocadoes and you were all set.

To start with, cars were a nightmare, at least for me: I had spent too many years wedged in my California pick up truck, and wanted to see what not having one would do for my body. In a bigger way, Hawaii was meant to be my exit strategy after twenty years in the US, so giving up my wheels was a step towards Eire in a different way – cars felt like anchors, sometimes, keeping you where they were.

Not to mention the other major, major details: the wild Hawaiian driving; the hectic Hawaiian traffic: the terrible, terrible Hawaiian parking. The noise, pollution, westernisation, laziness: they all seemed to go with my newfound, Zach-driven, anti-car culture. Plus, Oahu was a pretty small place, anyway: no need for seven-hour trips in to the desert, or associated equipment, out here.

So, no car, at least for now: live near work, live near the beach, live near a wave. That was all I wanted, as well as a few other nuances related to not liking heights or even living on the lower floors of big buildings – hard to find low-rise places in Waikiki, that is for sure, but eventually things worked out.

From the outside, the Aloha Punawai on Saratoga looks pretty out of place: part of a strip of 50's-era three story buildings in a town of towering skyscrapers, and sort of old school, and very low key – but I was stoked. I didn't want to live in a beehive, and wanted to be in touch with the world passing by: no way to do that from the 27th floor, at least not for me.

And so room 203 became, basically, a surf shack: a place with a bed and a small kitchen and bathroom and some furniture; a place that stored surfboards and had a lanai with no view at all, and a lot of noise from traffic, revellers, and neighbours passing through. A place that was low in rent – but also a place that most, if not all, would maybe feel wasn't right for them: a place with only the basics, that sort of fit with that surf-life ascetic aesthetic that I was trying to achieve. Who knew when I would need to tool up for more demanding parts of life, but either way the reductionist vibe seemed to relax me just then– no clutter, few possessions, and plenty of time to stretch, strengthen, and stay fit for surfing.

The boards took up position behind the small dining table; wetsuit (a modified long john, to be precise, both to hold my body together and protect from reef and sun) and shorts hung over a spot on the back balcony – sorry, lanai – to dry each day. There was a surf drawer containing wax, ding repair gear, and all the rest; there was a stack of surf mags in the cupboard. Even the fridge was based on a surfing diet: eggs, rice, pasta, sardines, avocadoes; soy sauce, grapefruit juice, chocolate, and all the rest: surfing fuel.

No pictures adorned the walls: the TV was never turned on. Like I said, pretty low key. At night, for sure, I would watch movies on the laptop (when not in the notorious Kelly O'Neill's) but not on a couch, oh no: lying, in true feral style, on a yoga mat looking up at it on the table, with folded towels as a pillow. In another corner, foam rollers, Therabands, and some weights. And no air conditioning, even though it was an option: one sheet on the bed, and the ceiling fan spinning, and it was good night Honolulu.

Outside the front door, a jacaranda tree bloomed all year round; often the flowers would fall on to my surfboard as I was waxing it up. The bed was soft, without sagging, which eased my body in the absence of a bath: in the evenings, or during the day, I would stall and talk story with Mike and Alden, the Hawaiian maintenance men: usually about surfing with Mike, and about fishing with Alden. The ladies who cleaned the other rooms and the receptionists all said hi; the neighbours would drop in dinner sometimes – there was a vague feeling of being included and accepted amidst the anonymity of a big new town. And at night, sometime, you would get that sound of the clinking of dishes from the kitchen at the back of the Breakers Hotel next door – sounds that sort of made you feel accompanied, and that I would never have gotten on some 27th floor.

And, each day, through my sliver of view, I had, straight away, pretty much the best barometer of what was happening down the road: in the post office car park, across from me, I was sensitised to look, straight away, for roof racks. After that I would see surfers, maybe: but how many? What kind of boards? Were there empty spaces, groups, locals? That check, probably, told me more than all the forecasts put together.

For whatever reason, my reading habits evolved as well: from the fiction and thriller realm, gradually that all fell away. A history of Hawaii got me into the groove, and led to other strange paths: for a lot of the time, the only books I could read were about polar explorers. Who knew why? Was it the descriptions of the cold that made you stop thinking about the heat; was it the chance to experience that same reductionism – that same living-close-to-nature kind of energy?

My room at the Pagoda was, after all, almost a polar hut, in the best possible way: there was the consolation, as well, and as a work colleague once said to me, of comparing hardship with hardship. Don't get me wrong, Hawaii was no prison, but rock fever could occasionally get a hold of you: I didn't know too many people, and was living a pretty minimalist existence. There were days when things didn't work out: but just one comparison with Nansen or Shackleton or Amundsen, living on their pemmican rations, would put it all into perspective.

Surfing in Hawaii

Not the same day that I met Zach at the showers, but a while after, I happened to be paddling out. There was Zach, somewhere ahead of me: as we approached the lineup, he was all smiles. On a greyish evening, there weren't many faces in the lineup – but those that were there, counted. 'That is Greg, that is Glenn", Zach said, sitting imperiously on his board and making some super-oblique introductions. Greg and Glen turned and nodded: they were, as they were always to be, midway along the lineup, in the bleachers. "And that is Ralph, Doug, Chuck, and Dave", he said, pointing to the top row – what I felt was the VIP area, but was in reality only for the very, very patient.

And that was surfing in Hawaii, at least for me: and I don't think anyone can understand it, until you have been there, which is probably what makes it the Mecca that it is: even South Africa, even California, even Australia, I was finding out, were just scratching the surface. Just the lemon beside the pie, just side shows: the obsessions, the dedications, the etiquette of all those places – the devotion and surf-lifestyles and identities – all paled in comparison with Hawaii.

To start with, in Hawaii, everyone surfs. Maybe it's the mayor, or the postman, or a professor, or a kid, or a great-grandfather: they are all out there. Not just that, but they are also doing more than just surfing: more than just competing for waves. Introductions are made, society functions, land translates into water and back again: reputations are made, characters are exposed; flaws are revealed.

I was getting to start to think of other theories, as well: the way the island's mood changed with the waves. Sometimes, there were waves on all coasts; other times, no waves anywhere. Was I imagining it, or was there a greater sense of ease in the water when there were waves everywhere – in particular after maybe a run of a week or surf? And was there a gloom, a surliness even, during the no wave times?

Not just all that, either: in Hawaii, in surfing, there are subtleties of etiquette and decorum that are almost unfathomable. Everything counts: the way you sit on your board, the length of your leash; whether you have a leash. The way you wax your board; what you say; where you sit: your posture; how fast you paddle back out. And, by the way, what route do you take to paddle back out – and who do you nod to and acknowledge along the way? And, hey, what as the expression on your face?

And more: even if you are in position, there are more than a few variables in play. When was your last wave: who is the old guy or the kid who has been waiting? Who has the moral right to the wave; who is not just in the right position in regards the ocean but in regards society – the lineup – karma? Who is the guy who has paddled out late because he has been working and you have been sucking up waves for the last hour – does he, maybe, get a right of way?

Gradually, and largely thanks to Zach and Mike, things became clear. The bull-in-a-China-shop energy that twenty-five years of global surfing still hadn't cured subsided: it was a good time to realise that just four top waves in a session wasn't a bad thing, but, even more importantly, that it wasn't about wave count anyway: that sacrifices now would pay back later on, in terms of patience and energy.

And so you grow: you learn attitudes to women, to the uncles, to the aunties, to kids. You learn to see good from bad; you learn to live with criminal moves, and watch as consequences unfold. You learn to hold your tongue and look away; you learn to intervene. But, above, all, you learn your limitations: learn to live with them, and learn to realise that you can aim not just to be the surfer who catches the best waves, or the most waves: in Hawaii, sometimes, when seeing behaviours degenerate and the waves get better, targets of spiritual optimisation and good vibes ascend in priority over the physical. There was, for sure, a lot going on.

Shoals of Time

Part of the spell, maybe, was in a book: some weeks later, getting slowly into the groove of Hawaii, under a tree, I read something called Shoals of Time. It was a book that mapped out, pretty much, the history of Hawaii since the dark ages; it was a hectic, hectic history, even by Irish standards: invasions and human sacrifices; inter-island wars and fratricides; nasty, nasty religions. Ancient gods that had good sides, for sure, but a little too much in the way of divine rights of kings: a little too much, maybe, of caste systems and cutthroat behaviours and putting people to the sword if they looked at you the wrong way.

So, under the tree, in the sun and in the shade, the Hawaiian birds sang and I took it in: read about missionaries and sugar barons and badly behaved sailors and Anglophilia; read about navies, and America, and de-possession and racism and coolies – and the way the place got to where it is today.

And, amidst all that, I would, all the time, put down the book and try to remember one thing the author wanted to get across: in some ways, in many ways – away from the military and the tourists and the mainlanders – Hawaii was strong enough, unique enough, and primal enough to always, always be itself. Not quite unconquerable, the way Ethiopia or Afghanistan or maybe Ireland were: but that thing was there, that key element, that *je ne sais quoi*, that renders a place timeless and raw and pure.

Kimo Time

With Kimo, you could never be too careful: his unreconstructed, blue collar political views didn't sit so well with the San Francisco dreaminess I was used to, and a visitor was occasionally treated to what might be considered a pretty full-on political treatise – in the shaping bay, or in the car to his shop, or pretty much anywhere.

I tried, as in work, as in everything, to stay out of it: all I wanted was the board, and Kimo was a burly, local, experienced Hawaiian shaper who wouldn't cost an arm or a leg or keep you waiting for six months – and who was referred to me direct by Mooch, a pretty heavy Rockpiles local, so I mainly just smiled and nodded when we talked. And Kimo was cool enough to let me sit in on the shaping sessions, and told me dodgy stories and shard the occasional re-heated taco, and talked about his divorces and girlfriends, and liked complements, and was for sure the real thing – but that was on the good days. Other times, I would get out to Sand Island and he wouldn't be in the mood for shaping, or would be resentful towards the universe about something or other: nothing would get done.

But I got the education, and we became mates: standing beside him, I watched as he turned blanks in to sculpture. Working out my body relative to Hawaii, and all the other variables, I had worked out that I needed something wide – twenty-four inches – and thick – four inches. Something not to long, say an offbeat length like a seven-seven or a seven-nine – a sort of all-rounder. If short boards were guitars, and long boards classical instruments, then I reckoned I needed a bass.

And something with volume through the nose and tail; something that would get in early, and fly. Something that most shapers would run away from: something that took more work and muscle and needed bigger blanks – and that maybe wasn't the most beautiful, sleek, svelte machine on the south shore. But Kimo was Kimo, and he was different, and he just didn't care, and neither did I, and so he shaped me my magic boards: emblazoned them with Irish and Hawaiian flags, and told me how to surf them, and set me on my way.

The Locals

Greg was a devotee, that was for sure. Rare not to see him out there, except maybe on the big days – and there was a very, very true and specific reason for that: he was, unfortunately, slightly too nice. Too patient and friendly and not a hustler on any level: content to be out there, and talk story, and shoot the breeze, and speculate on waves.

Content to go left and experiment with his numerous boards, many of which he had picked up at swap meets and thrift stores; content to laugh at any opportunity – content, basically, just to be there. Stoked to see the right waves come through and compare notes and make occasional *sotto voce* comments about the more eccentric ones among us; content to stick to his routines, and get his fair share of waves, and smile and laugh.

Don't get me wrong: he wasn't uncompetitive, and he could drop the hammer, the same as anyone – when people dropped in, or paddled around, or got in his way, or whatever. But, for better or worse, he also wasn't one for taking sides: when things melted down he would tend to observe and comment later – rather than necessarily backing anyone up, which is, probably, the best policy anyway. But even without that involvement he was a constant in a sea of changes – a regular and a local and a familiar face who would always give you the time of day.

Glenn had a similar vibe, but quieter: an uncle who wore his hat every day, and didn't seem to mind if he got waves, and only turned up on certain mellow days, and for sure occasionally paddled in to a nice one. He drove quote the beater, always had a story to tell, and was about as chill as you could be – letting the more hectic parts just wash over him, somehow.

And Skipper Dave, who knew the wave because he had sailed past it so many times in the Mai Tai tourist catamaran: stolid, occasionally a wave fiend, devotee of odd boards, philosopher, raconteur – all the ingredients you need for a life on the waves. And Doug, a pilot, who had a philosophical vibe and a moustache and a ponytail and plenty of stories – we would stand around watching the surf talking about bikes, and his time in the Coast Guard, and the waves, sometimes – and would wait for the wave he wanted, riding it switch stance, for even longer than Chuck. (Chuck was another story.)

And Ralph: the image of a Hawaiian local, sensitive and intense and sometimes prone to fits of laughter: and Rich, who owned the local catamaran business – and was built like a tank, and always work Hawaiian board shorts, and who had a handshake that would just totally envelop your hand, and who drove a low rider old school VW bus, and who could do headstands on his board when he felt like it. And Christina, a charging dentist lady who spoke with an East Coast twang and never, pretty much ever, backed down.

And Jon – a tall haole, like me – but, unlike me, a former lifeguard with deep Hawaiian roots, and a range of boards for every day, and always a good story: someone who would throw a good vibe your way, and had so many cool stories, and would review the cameras, and let you know if you hooked a good one. And Jason, who was friends with Michael, who came over from Southern California to surf in Hawaii once in a while: and Daniel, intense but fair, tetchy but approachable: and François, a Frenchman who surfed with style: and Nathan, who went left, and who would turn up once in a while.

And Art and Al, two old school mates who liked the lefts and the shoulders: and Tom, who shaped his own boards and always, gave you the time of day as he was scoping out a parking spot on Saratoga. And Trevor: a super stylist who rode the big days on a single fin; and Kyle, who sat wide and said "Go, brother!" when he saw you line up for a nice one. And Terry, a true surfer, who rode big old school boards on the lunchtime shift: and, amidst all that diversity, there was one thing they all had in common: they could surf.

Worth saying that, maybe: worth saying that they could all surf, because, lets face it, not everyone can. I mean, profiling those guys – south shore surfers – sure, maybe you could just sort of dismiss them as Bs, or Cs, in the surf rankings. But, no question, they weren't: because this was Hawaii, right? So Bs were As, Cs were Bs: the bar was higher, the standard was on another level, and if you didn't surf well, you weren't really at the races.

That, maybe, was the thing about Hawaii: people surfed super well. I mean, not just in terms of surfing – everyone had their limitations – but in terms of the details. No one who was anyone ever really paddled and missed: no one got caught too far out of position. Not one of those guys ever really fell off – rarely would you see one of them on a wave that wasn't the right one for them, at that moment in time.

And how lucky was I – right? I mean, sure, they weren't your best mates: by this stage of surfing, I, like them, had probably wised up to the fact that, yeah, you needed some boundaries with other surfers. I mean, don't go into business with them, right? Don't socialise too much, apart from the odd beer, or it can all go down in flames: don't, like, go on boat trips together, or live together, or anything. But, on the flip side – to be new to a place and have that kind of cast to shoot the breeze with, on water and on land? To pass the time of day and check the surf and laugh after good sessions and complain when it was flat? That was the surfing passport, right there, and I was, no question, super grateful for it.

And, one other thing: they loved their boards. Loved, loved, loved them: Chuck and his Brewers, and in particular his yellow one – but also the orange one, and the other yellow one, and a few others. And Zach and his green–railed Arakawas, and Glenn on his board that seemed to go better at Three's than any other: Tom and his self-shaped machines built on a long relationship with the place; and Trevor on his retro Lightning Bolt single fins. And everyone, pretty much, doing their thing, and talking about their boards, and other peoples' boards, and checking them out, and comparing – but, at the same time, no one really caring, too much, what anyone else thought, or rode.

And, yeah, on that exact note, before I forget, the foilers: the new school who got super long rides, and weren't really surfers, but got as close as you ever could to hanging with the surfers – Lyndsay, Ed, Anthony, Leigh, and a few others. And everyone else: the hotel surfers, who checked in to Three's like it was a hotel – and checked out again, and you never saw them again; the styling wahines, in giggling groups. The military hackers, and the aunties, and the uncles, and the couples: they were all there, or some of them, on any given day.

And there was nothing bad about them: it was more a case of they all, in one way or another, having reached their final destination. They were happy, rightfully, to chill and life this amazing life:

happy to reflect occasionally on the rest of the world. I wasn't, for better or for worse, there yet – but I sure admired those who were.

Somewhere in Between

I had read a few different books about surfing in Hawaii; some idyllic, some condemnatory. Andy Martin – a cool guy, who I had once corresponded with – wrote one called *Walking on Water,* which basically made Hawaii, and particularly the North Shore, sound like a kind of wild west surfing nirvana – complete with romance, glamour, adventure, adversaries, wipeouts.

Chas Smith, on the other hand, a book called *Welcome to Paradise, Now Go to Hell,* took a different angle – basically slamming a lot of Hawaii but also saying a lot of nice things – just maybe not necessarily slamming the things that needed to be slammed, and not necessarily, maybe, saying the right nice things about nice people, or the right nice things about nice things. Both, though, were cool guys; both had been captivated by Hawaii, and tried to work it out to the best of their ability, and helped me to get a handle on it all.

VIP Waves

Eventually, on a late evening, after a while, I found myself out there on my own. Spooked, of course. Goes without saying: scared of the distance from shore, of the Pacific, of the looming darkness. But, finally, there was opportunity: Finally, maybe, I was going to do something really, really cool: out here, on my own, I was going to catch the VIP waves.

And that is what happened: having watched the maestros, and having waited, and dialled in the shore markers, and having sat super deep for a long time – over near Greg, over on the left – and having taken off on barely-makeable waves a hundred times – and having done a thousand other things as well, the waves arrived. Outside, there was no one to watch out for – no one taking the ones you wanted – but also no one to line up against:

for what seemed like a long time, but was probably no more than twenty minutes, I scrabbled and repositioned and rode the more energetic pulses: the ones that reeled and lined up and peeled, until darkness descended. It was, for sure, the end of the beginning.

Guidance from Mike

Mike, who knew a lot, would come at things from a slightly different angle than Zach. He could speak good pidgin, had grown up surfing his whole life, was local, and had walked a few mean streets in his time, and was, basically, the quintessential Hawaiian surfer. He had been sponsored; been to jail; surfed big waves and fast waves; found a super spiritual path; didn't like leashes all that much – and knew all there needed to be known, at least for me.

We talked a lot: he lived at the other end of the building, and was the security and maintenance man for the Pagoda – and a lot of other things as well: in between his routines, we talked about philosophy, and surf, and history, and the waves that day, and upcoming swells, and how to deal with Hawaii. Because of his pedigree, it was sometimes hard to feel totally on the same page – I knew that if we weren't good mates, which we were, there could have been tension in a lineup, at a certain point in time, had we been sitting beside each other. Even as a grandfather, he could send people in if he wanted, or lose patience, or talk a little intensely for comfort, or whatever.

But he had also mellowed with age: he invited me along to his brother's funeral, and the speeches were like him: a lot of retrospectives, a lot of colour, a lot of talking story, a lot of events and challenges – but, in the end, a tale of redemption and spirituality and peace – despite the eternal temptation to do otherwise. When Mike had problems with a person, or a place, these days he wouldn't surf there for a while – almost as if the place, the circumstance, had been what had caused the problem; as if it were externalities, not spirit or emotion or mindset, that had precipitated him sending someone in, or whatever.

He took me to pay music with his brothers; showed me the best rinsing hose to use, hidden around the back of the building, after the surf. He backed me in fifty-fifty situations; let me in to my room when I was locked out; told me I was part of the 'ohana; encouraged me; and told me he has seen me on nice waves. He shared his cheap spicy Hawaiian hot dogs, and always invited me when he was going surfing elsewhere; greeted me in the lineup or in the beach, or wherever we met. I knew I could confide in him, and ask him for guidance – but also knew that with Mike, the less you cried, the more respect you got.

You Really Don't Want to Surf Here

First, most important, let me tell you, for sure, why you don't want to surf here: it is a hell paddle. It gets hella crowded, and there are better, emptier, more perfect waves, in cheaper and more exotic places, to be had. There are big, big fish: there are locals, and – did I mention this already?) – it get super, super crowded. You won't catch a wave on a regular board, and the lineup markers are tricky, and there are currents – and there are super sharp urchins and reef edges underneath.

And you will never get a parking spot anywhere near, and – even if you do – if you do you will pay for it, surfing with one eye on the clock. Even the traffic to get to the parking – even the wait for the parking itself – is absurd. And, if possible, you'll need pandemic conditions to break the ice – otherwise, all the slots in the line up are taken, broski. And, all the way along, there is searing sun and sensory overload – and that is just for starters.

But, what a wave. What a wave, what a wave. What a wave. In a sort of a way, it was a glitzy wave: people talked about, it tracked it. But it was far out to sea, so that sort of watered that down a bit – the Hawaii Hollywood that goes with a lot of surfing breaks. The cameras, the crew, the scene – it was there, for sure, but just maybe not as much.

Anyway, here is what would happen: The sight line for sets, for whatever reason, wasn't all that amazing. You didn't always get that much warning before the wave prepared itself to rise up and hit the reef – but you had enough notice, enough time, to paddle and position and line up and take a breath – that is for sure. "It is just so perfect", said Kimo to me one day.

Taking off – feeling the updraft from nowhere, even on windless days, on the bigger ones – also gave you time and space: it wasn't slow, but you could see the angle of the shoulder, most of the time. You could see a wall, or an immediate hollow section: you could see Diamond Head and the sky and the sea ahead. You could get up and set yourself up and choose to fade, or race to the shoulder, or something in between; you could smile for a moment when you knew, just knew, that you had hooked a good one, even before you were on it.

And the wall would stand up – if you got the tone and trim of your speed pumps just, just right – and the crowd would part. And the wave, on your side, rooting for you, would give you clues as to what it planned to do: where the sections were; if it would be hollow; how fast or slow it was going to break. And the greens and blues and dark blues and blacks would shimmer in the evening light; the board would let the wave energy through your feet. And the reef would appear benignly below the water, flying past, and you might hear a hoot.

"You never see yourself surfing", Chuck had said one day, sort of meditatively: and it was true, but you sure could see the other -, and you sure could see them see you. One of the lads at home had once talked about something called 'The Look': an exchange of glances between close mates that signalled a wild night ahead. Now, The Look was different: it could be you, eyes glued to the surfer racing down the line towards you, or it could be them: starry eyed or staring hard from the shoulder; maybe with another hoot bizarrely distorted by the wave shape: in those fractions of seconds (if there was more time, you weren't surfing fast enough) the wave and the surfer and the other surfer – the observer, observed, and process – were as close to a perfect, cosmic tringle of events as you could get.

It could rope! It could reel, undulate, detonate. It could fire, and cook, and line up.

It could slow down, halfway through, and the pitch out and speed up: it would give you time to set yourself up for its hollow section. Other dynamics, as well, helped to make this happen: it liked, the most, a southwest swell: maybe out of two hundred and twenty degrees or so, that would push right across the reef and throw up magnificent, elegant wide ones that the surfer had to sprint east to get to. On those ones, the wide and racy ones, the rider would go a long, long way: Disappearing from view behind the wall, appearing occasionally, and finally reappearing on the inside, near the boat channel, a long way away.

Taking people out was always a nightmare as a result: it seemed to sort of damage the intensity, or the experience, something like that. But, mainly, I was probably just being selfish: this wave will do that to you, Chuck told me. It will turn you inside out, and make you behave as you shouldn't: it will make you greedy, and you will just want more and more.

Others agreed: maybe it was the way it was where it was, so far out to sea. Maybe it was the way it had the deep-water channel beside it for the catamarans; maybe it was the way you never, or almost never, hit the bottom. Maybe that was what made Kelly Slater say that it was such a fun wave: maybe that is why Carissa Moore liked it, according to Chuck. Maybe that, as well, was why you would see James Jones out there on the big days, on his big colourful tuberider boards, looking impassive, and taking the good wide ones.

But Threes – yes, Threes – was an epitome, as well: or at least I thought it was, and, yeah, pretty much still do. Not everyone would agree, and that is ok: *chacun a son gout*; to each their own. But, to maybe try and convince people: there was a spectrum of waves on the slice of the south shore that I got involved with – and it ranged, in a cool geographical sort of way, from west to east: from Ala Moana bowls, where you had rippers; sort of stylists; people who took really, really good care of their grooming, their wax jobs, and their choice of boardshorts. Then you had Kaisers, where you found, in no kind of bad way, a lot of pretty hard men, a lot of tattoos, a lot of vibes.

Then you teleport over the water to the other side: to the east end of canoes and Queens – to classic boards and sponsored young longboarders looking for the spotlight, and Gidget, and Beach Boys sort of things. And then to Pops, where you can find the hackers, and then to Paradise, where you find something else, something good, something hidden – and then: in the heart of it all, but also way out on the edge, way out to sea – at least to me – and at the point, again, where all the circles, all the Venn diagrams meet – you get Threes: classic when it felt like it, high performance when it wanted to be. Vibey when it wanted to be: zany, challenging, tricky, and right at the heart of what surfing is, was, and will always be.

And, on that sort of note, with all that in mind – what about all those other forms of surfing, anyway? What is, like, the essence here? To some, sure, surfing has to include death defying waves, and shallow waves, and Pipeline, and Waimea, and the North Shore. To others, it has to include foamies, and SUPs, and whatever else. And, yeah, yes, for sure, it all counts: but the idea, I was thinking, is to get the parts of surfing that all those other circles in the Venn diagrams overlap with: the board, the wave, the rider. The elements of style and grace and poise and fitness. The open face; the thrill, the stoke, the silhouette of surfer on wave. Connecting with nature, totally – but not to do with warm or cold water, or wetsuits or no wetsuits, or a thousand other scales or options: and, yeah, here in the home of surfing, in Honolulu, I was finding, I reckoned, that same essence.

And there was more: not to exaggerate, but the wave seemed to have some fairy circle around it. The passing catamarans threw beers to surfers, and cheered good rides: when my mate Christian arrived, I turned to him in the lineup, and he looked – no joke, despite the real hard fact that he was in his fifties, – he looked, at Threes, as he sat on his board, stoked and with hair tousled, like a kid of, say, thirteen. He had that expression, that hair, those eyes, that vibe.

I loved it: loved it, loved it. To see eyes light up, and hear him say nice things said about the place: it felt like the culmination.

Because some waves are like that, as Chuck had said: some waves intoxicate, and get people to dream and behave in a different way. Some waves, basically, get written about: no offense, but there are waves that just don't get people inspired like that, that don't – for whatever reason – light that particular fire.

The wave was, in essence, majestic: a masterpiece. "Seven waves at Paradise is worth one here", said Greg. The exchange rate sounded harsh, but maybe he was right: even Rabbit Bartholomew, a surf demi-god, had apparently written an old surfer magazine article about it. The line up, or pecking order, or hierarchy, or whatever you want to call it, resembled nothing less than a regal dynasty, a monarchy, as a result: I know, at one stage or another how it felt to be first, second, third, and fourth in line to the throne – with all the ups and downs of each.

On certain days, its spell was so strong that you were, for sure, if not in the moment, then at least in the day, the evening, and the hour: the past was wiped out, the future was laughably irrelevant. What had been and what was to come both felt like sides of a mountain, and you were at the summit – I guess the aim is to get, in Zen terms, into the hour, minute, second, to truly be here now – but it wasn't a bad, non-assisted effort at oneness, presence, mindfulness.

So Threes – or Three's – or once apparently known as Trees, because of the huge palms lining up on the shore, or once apparently known as simples because you just dropped in and went – but provably just Threes, as it was the third break in a row and the furthest out anyway, way the best – yeah, Threes was possibly the best wave in Hawaii, some said, hidden in plain sight: in the heart of the city; for one reason or another – maybe the paddle, maybe the parking, maybe the relentless magnet of the North Shore – there were days when we would have a perfect point wave, that wasn't actually a point, all to ourselves.

Chuck

Here is how he did it, or how I think he did it: he sat, and waited. Waited, waited, waited. He looked at the sky, and at the horizon, and at the sunset when it came: looked at passing boats, and stretched his shoulder, and paddled with his hands while sitting up on the board to stay in position. Conversations would happen, and greetings exchanged: there would be humour, and occasional jokes, and whatever else.

And in surfing, as you probably know, there is something called getting sucked backwards, over the falls. It is pretty bad: pretty humiliating and unpleasant, and for sure, not at all graceful. It has to do with luck and timing, totally but mainly about skill – and, trust me, there is no more amusing, devastating sight that a surfer headed for the meat grinder, upside down and backwards. And that sort of thing is pretty much exactly, precisely, what never, ever, happened to Chuck – ever.

Chuck was very, very chill: very skinny, very light, very fit. Very patient, very good-natured, and very wise: he had been surfing the wave, no joke, for nearly half a century. And he was bronzed by the sun, and was wiry and agile in a sort of ninja kind of way. A lover of Brewer boards, he was a stylist, and was the king of the wave, and made intricate rock creations on the beach, and was a valet on the dawn patrol at the Moana Surfrider so he could surf the evenings, and was a mellow cruiser: but, make no mistake, he would charge as well. But, mostly, he waited, and stated at the horizon, and shot the breeze, and waited, waited, waited.

Then, somewhere, an alarm would sound: a sixth sense would kick in. What was it? Was it just that there hadn't been waves for a while, and one was due about now? Was it a secret indicator, down towards Diamond Head? Was it a gamble, a hunch, or a technical – even an academic – decision? What told him where to go, every time?

Who knew: at the appointed time, Chuck would paddle, maybe for a wide one, and he would be in position. Like no one else, I mean: he would be outside, or at the top of the point, and would be at that exact, exact point and place where you needed to be. And from there it was a symphony, a maestro in action, poetry in motion: to see Chuck on the wave of the day, which he usually got, wasn't painful at all.

And, luckily, he backed me: maybe it was the Covid, maybe it was the lockdown, or maybe it was a phase he was going through or coming out of – or maybe it was something else. But, mostly, he backed me, and advised: one day, pretty soon after my first experience of the more sublime waves at Threes, another swell came through. Chuck was watching from Paradise as I hooked a few, and quickly paddled over to get some himself: "Those", he said to me on arrival, "were the best waves you have caught here so far". It was more than a complement: it was acceptance – from a guy who had caught his first wave there the year I was born – and that, in Hawaii, is what it is all about.

Surf Names

Amidst all of the absurdities and contradictions, one stood out more than others: for whatever reason, I had introduced myself to Zach as Sebastian. And that was it: for ever more, pretty much every surfer in Hawaii, apart from Cunningham, called me Sebastian. It was always that way: once someone gets that name hard wired, (probably like any other name, I guess), they won't switch back.

By contrast – and here it reached the realms of Alice in Wonderland, at least to me – the military people I worked with didn't like a name that long, so immediately shortened it to Bass – which was what pretty much any surfer in the Emerald Isle would call me. But, also, in a way, it was also a reflection of Hawaii: with plenty of long names in the surfing community (and not just Hawaiian ones – there were plenty of Napoleons, Nelsons, and Dukes in the water, for whatever reasons), it was another way of reflecting the formality with which surfing itself was treated. At the other extreme, the cool but slightly dehumanising call sign military vibe, where polysyllabic words were discouraged anyway.

Surfing was a different realm: a thing of beauty and class; a thing of elegance; something which was, for short moments of time, the preserve of all that is most refined in ourselves. Nominative determination, and politesse, and etiquette: that at least, that was the idea.

The Saratoga Walk

Even the walk to the surf had its own element of ritual. Strolling down Saratoga Road, a relatively quiet place by Waikiki standards, there was a handy grass verge that took pressure, and heat, off the feet. That, for sure, was a priority in Hawaii – a place where, even in winter, you could fry an egg on the sidewalk. A place where, whatever Mark Twain said about San Francisco, the hottest summer you were ever likely to spend was a winter in Honolulu: a place where humans, like animals, veered from patch of shade to patch of shade in the noonday heat; a place where the evening surf session ruled supreme, dodging glare on the eyes from the water and bodily dehydration from the heat.

Anyway, the walk: exit the Pagoda, stop for traffic, slip across. Not advised, especially as it is against the law in Hawaii, and I saw quite a few people getting ticketed for jaywalking. One time, doing my usual thing, I made the mistake – even though it was a sleepy intersection – of crossing under the eye of the HPD. The lady driving the car didn't stop, only slowed down: "Hey you… yeah, you…. Don't let me see you doing that again!" Talk about the spirit of the law: others found it funny, at the time, but I made sure that my new routine, not changed since childhood, now read: look left, look right, look for HPD, cross. So, I guess it had some effect; good for her.

Anyway, the walk: past towering skyscrapers, beneath palm trees: meeting familiar faces along the way, and maybe getting a super staccato surf report from someone going in the opposite direction. Nothing explicit, just a few words to the effect of "Yes, brah", or "No waves, brah" or "You'll have fun", or "Good luck".

And the locals: at the start of the grass verge, I would shoot the breeze with Mike, who had his own rituals: I never knew his full back story, but knew he had spent some time in Thailand; lived through hard times as well; and now had two sons who surfed a lot, one of them a pro longboarder, going under the *nom de guerre* of Johnny the Ripper.

Hawaii, I would reflect as I walked down Saratoga, was, if nothing else, a creature of habit: a sleepy enough place to allow for fine-tuning and refinement of personal systems: whether it was Mike in his car, or Chuck out the back, or the person in the park who sunbathed in the same spot on the same days, it was, in some kind of way, reassuringly routine.

In Bali, surfing Kuta Reef many years before, I had been blown away that you could lust leave your things on the beach and no one would take them. Here, now, in urban Hawaii, I was discovering that same sort of scene – down at the beach, eventually, there was usually time for just the basics, as I was usually, meaning always, running late: a word from the beach boys, bury the keys in the sand, put on the leash, say a prayer for protection, check the time, and hit the water.

So, eventually, you got to know pretty much everyone. Everyone had time to chat, as well, because this was Hawaii, and not New York: everyone had time to compare notes on the surf, and whatever else was going on. Usually – trying to swim or surf in the late evening to avoid the sun – I would leave maybe an extra ten minutes for the walk down to the beach, and still get there late: almost always, would hang back and chill with whatever familiar face walked by: would get buttonholed, on the sidewalk or on the sand, by those who lived similar routines to your own.

Later, after dark on the way back – even Neil, the late-night saxophone payer who was just stating hiss shift would say hello – in moments of stoke or flights of fancy, I would see the 42 bus. At night, cruising down Saratoga like a spaceship, it reminded of a series of books that said that the number 42 was, in fact, the ultimate answer to life and the universe and everything: was this life, I wondered, the ultimate answer? Well, maybe it was, for a while, even though ultimate answers tend to change.

"That Is Due South"

Chuck, above all, always – almost always – remained unruffled. Not quite stoic, but someone, you reckoned, who had seen it all: every wave, from every angle. He had started surfing the wave the same year I was born: he had, without question, a relationship with the place. A knowledge, an appreciation, an understanding – even an occasional friendly, affectionate contempt.

In carefully chosen words, on good days, he would describe the uniqueness of the wave: how it let you in, and showed you what was up ahead; how, on the more perfect days it was a long, roping, winding wall. How the wrong ones could catch you out with a section halfway; how the right ones would, at that same point, wall up and curl over and frame Diamond Head in the distance. But the key to it all, Chuck said, was not wind, or tide, or swell size: it was direction.

Direction, direction, direction: apart from loose boards and misplaced bodies and weaving through crowds on busy, big days, this was Chuck's one big, big thing. Where was south? He would ask me. "Not where you think it is", he would say, before I could answer. "Nowhere near."

Town, as the locals called Honolulu, could be deceptive: what looked like south, due to the angle of the coast, was actually south-west. "South is over there", Chuck would say, pointing into the distance and slicing the sky up and down with his hand, just to really emphasise the point. "Not over there. Look at the sun".

He must have said it to me a hundred times: "South is over there". But, he was right: it made all the difference. Caught in the wrong spot on a swell with too much east in it, you could find yourself hopelessly behind the section; sit too deep on a south-west swell and the waves would pass you right by, roaming across before breaking over the west end of the reef. I watched, and listened, and eventually it sank in: I was able to position myself, now, via a whole new range of vectors, and not just use the buildings as shore markers to line myself up.

It wasn't really a big deal: knowing where south was, and remembering it, and using the knowledge. And, yet, it sort of was: when the swells hit, and when the crowds came, it was another trick up the rash guard sleeve; another hidden advantage. And observing it – noting the direction, and the compass – was also, maybe, a sign of respect: a way of saying that you were listening, and were humble enough, most of the time, to admit when you had lost your bearings.

The Beach Boys

The beach boys had their own groove – and it was, like a lot of things in surfing, and a lot of things in surfing in Hawaii, a sort of mixture of the surreal and the seriously real. Mitch and Ryan and Grayson and Chase and Trevor manned the beach umbrella and sundeck station: they scanned the surf each day, and welcomed you, and dismissed you, and got busy and got slow, and shot the breeze, and filled you in on the latest events.

It was, essentially, beach life: they would track tides and swells and bikinis and strange pieces of flotsam; checking the crowds, and the boats, and the vibes, and any possible other unusual thing that might pass across their ultra-local transom – from a broken shower head to a sniffing dog, to water quality to Chuck's intricate rock sculptures on the sea wall, to the characters of characters of the lineup. And they knew a few other things, as well: the coming and goings on the beach; who did what; who was where. It all registered, amidst the other local lore they picked up: which hotels were haunted, on which floors, and why: the ghosts they had seen late at night when working other gigs around town.

So much for the cinematic side: so much for the lads who lived and worked on the beach under the blazing sun, and drank beers from paper bags together after work, and shared them with you, and who skated home after the end of day session. Sunglasses clapped to their eyes, and beauty all around them, oh yeah: the beach boys really existed, and really loved it, even though there were realities.

The realities of the blazing sun, and hard conditions, and work that could strain the body, and battles over fair wages, and whatever else: the lurking feeling that it wasn't going to last forever sometimes surfaced, but was countered by the love they had for what they were doing: like me, like Peter Pan, they were in no rush to grow up and leave the beach and move to the suburbs, or whatever else. Just a bit longer, just another year: the Pump House Gang made real, under the Honolulu sun.

And the strange thing was that the beach, which was what it was all meant to revolve around, wasn't actually that amazing. No offense, no offense. You would think it would have been – the hub, the focus, the start and the finish and everything in between in Hawaii. And in a way it was – at the tables near the showers, at the showers, in the water, at the beach boys stand. But the beach, *qua* beach? The sand? The thing was, there wasn't much of it.

There used to be, for sure: you could see it in the photos. But things had changed, for whatever reason. The strip of sand was, probably, maybe two to five yards wide in most places near the showers. And, not just that: as soon as you got into the water, the sand disappeared – boom! Straight on to the reef, mate. Sharp, shallow reef: blame climate change, blame the volcano: curse its treacherousness, but just don't get cut.

And so we would chill, there, between the tourists and the reef, and I would get the latest from Mitch, and even gamble occasionally for the Friday evening tip jar: the lads would fold the big tip, say a ten-dollar bill, and flip it in the air and bet on which way it would land. I never won, but felt honoured to be involved: the beach boys didn't have time for every blow in. The privileges of sharing occasional beers flowed also with gratis storage of valuables (as close as I ever got to the days on Kuta Beach, twenty years before, when I could leave my flip flops on the sand, go surfing, and come back and find them) and their keeping an eye out for lost boards, and discussing Zach's eccentricities, and whatever else: when there was no one else around, the lads made me welcome, and showed me the ropes.

'Waves when there Ain't'

One thing was for sure – everyone hated the forecasts. Surfline, or whoever, drew crowds, and seemed to get it wrong almost all of the time – overcalling it to protect themselves from liability, maybe – but also maybe because waves are good for business, right? I mean, thinking about it all: who would be a surf forecaster? You wouldn't wish it on your worst enemy, even though it seemed like it could be a profitable gig as well.

Chuck had his own thoughts, and, like they usually were, they were good ones. "Look out of your window", he would recommend when people asked him what the waves might be like: "Walk to the beach". He was almost offended, sometimes, when people said to him that there would be waves tomorrow. "Tomorrow is another day", which for sure it was – but it was also an acknowledgement that neither the forecasters, nor the rumongers,, nor the clairvoyants, would ever – ever – get it right. Not only that, it was better when they didn't: that would lead, sometimes, to the most magical of days; the late evenings when a pulse would come in unexpectedly, and there would only be just a handful of contenders there.

"Waves when there ain't", was Chuck's quasi–Wild West way of summing it all up. The South Pacific is a big place, let's face it, and even the forecasters sometimes acknowledged what they called SOUOs – swells of unknown origin. Like something out of Conrad, and even in the tech-riddled 21st century, strange rhythms and unseen storms could still send in mysto swells, and beat the forecasters, and reward the devotee.

The All-Americans

No question, Hawaii was out there; no question, Hawaii was not America. A lot of Hawaiians, even though Americans themselves, sort of subscribed to that: sort of said, hey, this isn't really what we are about, or where we are from, because we reckon this is better in pretty much every way. Technically, there was a nuance as well: sure, it was a united state, but it wasn't America: wasn't the continent and the mainland, by name or by nature.

One thing, though, was that you would, whether you liked it or not, get all forms of mainlanders there: because of the tourism – and in such a polarised and compartmentalised country – in some sort of strange way, you got to see everyone, all the time. Out in Hawaii, the tourists came from everywhere: in California, maybe, you were only exposed to the Californians, and sort of missed out on how everyone else was thinking or feeling.

Here, you met the Floridians and the South Dakotans, the Montanans and the New Yorkers and the Texans. Alabama, Alaska – they were all there: peering through hotel windows and staring at the sea and not always looking that healthy, but whatever: this was their moment in the sun, their big two weeks, the time to forget about how much they spent to get there, and what their budget was, and all of those heavy things.

And you know what? Generally, they were good people. For sure, there were extremists, and people with some pretty strange ideas – but, at the end of the day, your average American on holiday in Hawaii was just your average American: pretty easy going, pretty fond of a drink in the evening, pretty die hard in terms of politics – but still humans, and normal, and all the rest. It was harder, basically to vilify the proverbial other, the nameless and faceless from over there: you weren't separated by thousands of miles of freeways and prairies; you were face to face, and maybe even saw a bit of yourself, to your surprise, in who you met.

The Eco Warrior

On one occasion, a plastic floater – some kind of tourist-bobbing ring – drifted past the lineup. It was, as far as I can remember, me and Skipper Dave and Greg out every night. In line with the mood of the day – grey skies, light winds, long waits – we dumbly watched it drift by, headed in to open ocean. That, it seemed like, was that. A plastic interlude, nothing more.

What we hadn't accounted for, though, was Zach. For sure, I had some edgy thoughts about the plastic, after having attended my share of Surfrider meetings. I mean, I was washing and re-using plastic forks at the time, just to be good – but, flip side, we were, like, ten minutes paddle from shore, and there was no way anyone was going to hold on to the thing while trying to surf. Polishing my halo, I made a silent vow to pick up an equal number of pieces of beach litter when I got back to shore – that evened it out, karma-wise, right? – and got back to scanning the horizon.

So much for that idea: paddling out, super late as usual, Zach had witnessed – he would likely say borne witness, just to dramatise it – to the whole episode. I was still new, and told him my plan straight away, so got out of the line of fire. But for Greg and Dave's benefit, he made some loud remarks about protecting the ocean, respecting the turtles, and other aspects of environmentalism. He then said it all again, louder – testier; getting himself worked up. The lads, used to it, didn't seem to notice.

Yet the episode, even then, wasn't over: Zach wanted waves, but he also wanted to save the planet – but, he also wanted waves. So there was only one solution – only one thing to do, that also allowed for tide and current: periodically, he would paddle to the ring, paddle inside, and sit it in the middle of the lineup. The wind had slackened, going into evening, so that helped: but, every now and again, it would creep outside, and he would repeat the process. At one point, while working out his next move, he attempted to surf while actually wearing the grotesque and now half-deflated object – wrapping it around his waist while sitting on his board – and that is an image, trust me, that will stay with you.

Eventually, he won, as he always did: against tide, wind, people, nature, whatever; *contra mundum.* Meeting him on back on the beach in the dark, I followed through with my pledge and picked up whatever flotsam I could find – some abandoned high heels; a few plastic drinks cups; whatever else – and put it in the bin. Appeased, if not quite approving, the episode blew over. I was still in the good books – for now.

Kelly's and Arnold's

Pretty much, as far as I could ever see, every Irish expatriate or rover, or whatever you want to call him or her, gravitates towards the local Irish pub from time to time. It was a cliché and a stereotype and an archetype, for sure – and the Murphia had lived that to the hilt, through and through, in California – but

Hawaii was going to be different, right? A different ethos, place, environment: far from the Irish lads and the structures – social and anthropological – that drew the Irish back in to the pub.

Maybe, maybe not: Kelly O'Neill's, a pretty much notorious late bar in the heart of Waikiki, was also the soul of the place: a not too lavish, low brow, warm, noisy, and occasionally violent melting pot. A place for drunken tourists, drunken military, and drunken locals: but a place, also, for a mellow glass of wine after the waves, listening to whoever as playing guitar that night.

Pretty soon, I knew the musicians pretty well, and got a nod from them as I walked through the door. After past lives involving wild excess, I kept it real and found just one glass of vino and a soda water would settle things down and set the tone for another warm, dulcet evening in Honolulu. The barmen would put the surfing on the TV if I asked, and the music would play, and the day's waves would be reviewed – either solo, or with whoever was around.

In other ways, Kelly's – and Arnold's, an even more surf-oriented spot around the corner, complete and replete with surfboards hanging from the ceiling – fit in and developed, in different ways, with the surfing life. For one thing, there would be days, on the first big south swells I encountered, when things would get slightly out of control: days when the post-surf shower, and stretch, would have to hang fire for a little while: days when adrenaline would dominate proceedings, and I would go from ocean to pub, pretty much direct. Days when the red wine would switch to white, and one glass would change to three, as I gradually came down to earth from the celestial heights of the waves.

More than that, Kelly's and Arnold's were, almost, private members' clubs: a place to retire and feel at home when beaus and dogs and other things that sustained were far away. An embrace, in a way, at the end of the day: places with noise and life and notoriety. But, for sure, the question remained, for better or for worse, in a good way or in a bad way: how had it come to this?

Rewind I: Goodbye San Francisco

Sunset at Ocean Beach, San Francisco.

The End

Before you start in Hawaii, other things have to end. And there is a line, in a scene, in a movie – there is this one specific scene that captures the essence of what I am trying to say better than anything else ever could, even though it has nothing to do with surfing, and nothing to do with Hawaii. It is a great, great movie – you have to see it. And, for some reason, this line, in the one particular scene, in this one movie, just summed it all up: a man – in this case a football manager – is standing outside a boardroom door, in a corridor.

He is staring at the door: the viewer knows that deliberations about his performance, future, are taking place inside. He is staring at the door, but has the thousand-mile stare: At that point, one of his mates – one of his allies – walks around the corner, and sees him, and asks him what is happening: why is he staring at the door? "What's happening, boss?", he says. And the manager, still staring at the door, says: "What is happening, Jimmy, is the last two words in every story ever written in the English language, ever: The End."

Not to dramatise it, in any way, but that was what was happening to my life, and therefore my surfing life, in San Francisco: it was hard to imagine life without Ocean Beach, but the end was what was coming down the track, that was for sure. Over the years I had often wondered what the last session would be like, and equally what my final withdrawal from Cali would manifest itself as: I had seen them in all shapes and sizes, over the years.

Most of the time, it was with a whimper: off to buy a house somewhere cheaper, or go home, or whatever. But it was always, always gnarly: no one ever seemed to leave with their head held high, proud of what they had done. Instead, everyone seemed to just want more and more of SF; or saw the place as totally unique;

or thought any place else would be a backwards step; or that they had somehow failed by not going down the tech route; or whatever.

I didn't want to go down that road. Last time I had left – to go and live and surf in South Africa for a few years – yeah, I had pined for it, for sure. The departure wasn't really all that clean: too many drunken nights, too lugubrious. This time, I wasn't going to do it that way: maybe I wanted to leave the place the only way a surfer ever really should – by heading to a place with more, and better, waves; by going to Hawaii.

One thing that was going to help me, I was realising, was Ocean Beach itself: in most surf spots, you have a relationship, of some kind, with your fellow surfers. You have car park or surf check chats; sometimes you get into texting, or nights out, or parties, or whatever. Everything, socially, forged and linked by waves: by tricky situations, and moments of glory, and mutual comparisons and respect. It is hard, for sure, to leave any such crew – you spend some of life's best moments with them.

Ocean Beach, almost uniquely, wasn't like that: like so much of SF, there was an element of anomaly, or differentiation, even in the ocean. For OB, I had figured out, it was the way you had a relationship with the beach, the tides, the surf, the pelicans, and the dolphins – even the weather – but rarely, if ever, with your fellow surfers. It was too long, too spread out; there were too many currents, too much longshore drift: too many shifting peaks that you paddled towards until, like mirages, they retreated just as you got close.

Even with your mates, it was rare that you would spend the whole session together: fog would descend, or a long ride would intervene, or someone would paddle one way and someone else the other way. All you could hope for, most of the time, was to get together back in the car park at some kind of mutually acceptable time. (That didn't always happen: the sand dunes at OB were often dotted with surfers looking balefully out to sea for their mates with the car keys).

But – like I was saying – when it came to the crunch, D-Day, SF's last session, it wasn't that hard: an easy release, without much concern about how you would miss the camaraderie, or the waves, or whatever, the next day. Maybe that in itself was something to be thankful for: too often, surfing taps into habits and routines and makes departures painfully melancholy. On the other hand, there were still moments to come that could be recalled with a mixture of amusement and absurdity....

Big Red

Aimlessly, Jan and I watched the surf. It was too big for us, and too big for most people, and too big for pretty much everyone, actually. As a result, there was a lot of lounging, and surf checking, and checking other surfers checking the surf, going on down at the end of Noriega Avenue, up on the sand dunes.

Amidst the few who were out there on a bombing day – a day you wouldn't really want to touch – was one surfer on a huge red gun. Immediately we christened him Big Red as we watched him – or her – paddle for bomber after bomber. On a sheet-grey, steely day, Big Red made it look easy: paddling in to waves and dropping almost vertically, relying on the glassy conditions for the time and space to fly down the line.

The significance, if there was any, and the memorable element, was maybe the shadow line – the way we just accepted that this person was out there going big, and we weren't. We had both been schooled often enough at OB to know that, even with the testosterone and the laddishness and the camaraderie and the desire to go bigger than you had before – or at least bigger than your mates were going – there was still a limit. A line that you would willingly not cross, and not even fret about not crossing; a line that let you just sit back and enjoy the show.

The Fog

Just when you think you know a place –when you have studied it from every angle, on every kind of day, over maybe a decade

– just when you think you have got a spot dialled, and have seen it at its biggest and its smallest, its best and its worst, then something new comes along. In this case, a fog-bound OB session that defined, even redefined, ethereal – if that is the right word.

Jan was keen, and that was good, because it wasn't the kind of day you would have gone alone: you couldn't even see the waves from the beach, and OB was, if not forbidding, then at least a little spooky. But time was running out: I knew my SF life was drawing to a close, so a lot of the filters were disposed of. Lucky that they were: upon getting out the back, we saw maybe four, maybe five others, sharing a surreal, fog-bound, grey-and-silver, ultra, ultra-glassy peak.

At OB, you tend to get separated anyway, though on this case we all stuck pretty close together. An Asian lady on a longboard was finding lefts and rights; others were seeking bigger ones further out. But, wherever you were, there was one common denominator: The waves stood up in a mirror-like wall, and peeled, and then peeled and peeled and peeled some more.

Flickering in and out of each others lines of vision, I guess we must have seen each others' rides, but it was more about the setting than the surf: more about the kind of uniquely San Francisco quality to the situation. It was so surreal, so Grateful Dead, so Ken Kesey – so psychedelic, but without the pharmaceuticals and hallucinogenics – that you couldn't have made it up.

The Dolphins

At the end of one era, and the star of another, things were starting to unravel. I knew, in my soul, that the years in SF were over, and that they were probably not going to end beautifully – in my experience, they rarely did. At the end of the tether, and yet still attached, the moment had arrived that I had always wondered about: the last drive down, through the park, to OB.

In reality, it wasn't anything special: too much angst, and onshore winds, and the wrong tide, and indifferent waves all added up to a forgettable session. I looked around, and saw the skyline one more time: looked out to sea, and maybe saw the Farallons in the distance. The surf had its usual therapeutic effect – though I knew the game was up, for sure, and even the ocean's embrace couldn't dislodge the pathos.

But, as if on cue – OB did remember it's faithful, I guess – a pod of dolphins popped up and cruised by. They wheeled and cruised and that was it: nothing special, nothing out of the ordinary – just a very casual salute to make me feel better, maybe, and little but of a farewell. I didn't surf there again for a long, long time.

Hawaii 2: Salmon Sunsets

View from the siesta.

Playing Cards and Salmon Sunsets

Some days, even in Hawaii, no waves came in at all. "What are they doing out there?" I asked Greg as we watched the lineup from shore. "Playing cards", he replied laconically, laughing: it was true, I guess. All that was lacking were the cards themselves, and a table, and a smoky haze: apart from that, it was the same shoot-the breeze, reflect on life, talk-about-whatever kind of vibe.

Occasionally, fits of imagination would replace history lessons or local news observations. "These are salmon sunsets", Chuck said one evening, "over a silver sea". That was true, as well: the waves were shining under a deep, deep orange set of clouds as the sun lowered over the horizon. The title was too long for the book – which was what he was thinking about – but the sentiment was right: that was, on most days, what it was all about.

The Kewalos Run

Eventually, I started running again, just for the sake of it. For the first six months, it was unthinkable: I would see people going for jogs in the Hawaiian heat and think, "wow, that looks so unhealthy". And, for sure, it could be: dehydration; sun burn; lazy muscles: tourists stepping in your way; holes in the pavement; traffic. But if you needed to sweat out the night before, or somehow decompress before a big surf session, it was the best way.

The route itself was surf-rich: past Three's and Four's and Kaisers and Rockpiles; over the bridge past Bowls and along Magic Island to a wave Mike called the Bombora. And along Ala Moana Beach Park, in all its sunlit, local kine, barbeque-smoke glory: past tents of Samoans with their sound systems, and locals with Defend Hawaii flags or traditional emblems from royal family days. Past kids and old people and cook outs and sound systems;

past surfers and surf spots – Courts, Concessions, Shallows, and the rest.

And, eventually, to Kewalos, and the end of the line: to the local fishermen who always said hi, always said "nice weekend" – to the grommets ripping by the harbour mouth, and sunlit views of the bodysurfing magic of Point Panic across the inlet. To the westernmost boundary of my life – and to the stature of the owl.

The owl was cool: my one local god, its outspanned wings oversaw a plaque commemorating an ancient battle in which a man – a local who had been kind to an owl in distress – had later been rescued by the owl and his friends. The word was 'amakua – protector – and I knew I needed as much of that as I could find.

A Word from Tom

Too often, life spills over into surf. It becomes an escape, at first, but until something happens – a wave or a greeting or a moment of reflection, maybe – you are still carrying the day's woes with you. On such an occasion, a word from Tom, one of the elder statesmen of the pack, did the trick. It wasn't anything significant – maybe just "nice wave", or "nice to be out here", or something like that – but the change was made: the clouds parted, and surfing had fixed things once again.

The HCC

Even with surfing, and even with surfing in Hawaii, it seemed there had to be a foil: something to contrast it with, and set surfing against – something like cricket. Something, I found out, like the Honolulu Cricket Club: something to take me out of my rarefied niche; something to put surfing, and its pleasures and pains and privileges, into perspective. No better contrast, no better *amuse-bouche,* than six hours of hyper-competitive humiliation on a Sunday, on the blazing hot heath of Kapiolani Park, with a demented selection of – mainly – good-natured cricketers.

It was, I was learning, a club in decline, if not in crisis – but there was a hard core of Indians, Sri Lankans, and Nepalese who kept that colonial relic, the oldest cricket club in the South Pacific, in business. There was also politics, bouncers, arguments aplenty, injuries, shouting matches – and, above all, moments of extreme humility as I was out for another duck, or as my bowling was sprayed around the ground.

The HCC taught me a few other things, as well: Kishore, a Nepalese, had a way of acknowledging and agreeing through a wave of his hand, that pretty much defused any situation. It was a wave, and a sign to chill out, and a message that said don't worry, we are on the case.

The other thing, maybe, that the HCC represented was the modern Hawaii: most of these guys, like I said, were Indian or Sri Lankan or Nepalese: Johannes was a Boer, and Clarence was from Zimbabwe. There were West Indians, as well – and there were elements that hadn't been present in the South Pacific ever before. There was the global tech migrant professional class; there was globalisation, to add to the already super diverse Hawaiian society.

But, yeah, Hawaii, for sure, was already diverse – so it was just another layer: a new demographic, with its own bubbles and dynamics and hang ups and issues. The only thing that was missing amidst this 21st century melting pot was, ironically, the Irish: it seemed like, with the odd exception, the long arm of the Emerald Isle pretty much stopped at California: San Francisco had been an Irish town in parts; Honolulu, apart from the pubs, couldn't really claim it. Was it that the Irish just didn't want to live on islands, or something? That we got intoxicated by mainlands?

Anyway: away from all that, away from the cricket, just hours later I would be back in my element: it was around then, maybe, that I knew for sure, after twenty-five years, that surfing was for me. I had often doubted it – doubted my skills, and physique, and wondered if the sacrifices it had demanded were ever going to pay off, and all the rest – but now, for sure, as I glided into another right hander and compared it to my cricket performance, I knew, knew, knew.

Full Moon Fever

Often, you couldn't make it up. With Zach, and one or two others, on a summer full moon, which rose right over the tip of Diamond Head, we surfed in to the dark. I noticed a noble-looking grey-haired gent hooking a few, but thought nothing of it until Zach paddled up: "You are out today with a legend", he told me. He said, quietly, it was Mark Cunningham, the North Shore lifeguard, and told me to behave accordingly. A modest soul, Mark had saved a lot of people and a lot of surfers, despite his apparent indifference towards the breed – "Surfers are a motley crew", he later said to me.

But, that was later: right now I just paddled up, and introduced myself, and said that anyone who did good things with their lives for not much reward was, to me, riding pretty high in the karma stakes. He brushed it aside, but was also friendly; we talked about Ireland, and his Irish DNA, and a contest there in 2001 that we had both attended – even standing in the same room at one point. Thus the quirks of time, and place, in the surfing universe.

Anyway: the moon rose. We surfed. All was good. We laughed. We talked about Ireland; murderous shouts arose from the direction of paradise. We surfed some more; the moon rose higher; the murderous shouts rose in volume and gained in proximity. The moon rose even more; we surfed; it was dark. The shouts reached a crescendo: threats to kill from an unknown source, spookily reaching our ears.

The passion of the shouting was hectic, but not knowing who the person was talking to, or where they were in the darkness, was worse. Mark's lifeguarding instinct pricked up – but he had seen it all. Even though he had rescued a lot of crazy, drugged-out people over the years, he also had the wisdom to know that there was danger afoot – not least when there was no chance of seeing where they were in the moonlit darkness. There were invisible lines in the lifeguard's world, it seemed like, even when retired.

Eventually the lunatic, and his manic cries, receded into the night – but the surf session was indelibly affected, like it always is, with the trespass of land or of distress. I guessed that the wildness of Waikiki had once again permeated the ocean, which was rare but inevitable: how could you have so much strangeness on land without it occasionally trespassing into the sacred preserves of the sea? At the showers, Zach laughed; it had made his night.

Hard Edges

Gradually, inevitably, the honeymoon ended. I knew it not just from text messages from Zach to that effect, but also from the days, here and there, when bigger swells started to roll in. Odd faces started to appear – not tourists or non-locals: no, no, no. *Au contraire*: the deep locals who only turned up – due to age or travel or whatever else – on the days when it looked good. The days when Eddie, a wiry and mellow Hawaiian elder statesman, came out, and, also – when bigger – when the North Shore guys, including James Jones, came to town, gracing the line up with their presence.

I, on the other hand, even after twenty years of surfing, was still greedy, still new, and still pretty innocent. Still high on the magic of Hawaiian waves: still judging Hawaiian surf by the standards of behaviour, the expectations, of pretty much anywhere else on the planet. But Hawaii was different: more sensitive, more subtle, more gradated. Even small days aroused emotions if conditions were good enough; the J-Bay locals, even, didn't have that dimension to their surf-social dynamics.

It was best represented, as always, by Zach: by his paddling out on one of those days and sitting beside me – but, for once, not talking: looking over with a hint of disdain, a hint of warning, and no reply to the usual repartee beyond a grunt. It came as a shock, but not an unwelcome one: better to get mildly vibed by someone whose heart was in the right place than by a stranger – right?

It was, maybe, his way of being good, fair, even kind; a Hawaiian surfing form of tough love, and it was clear he was nervous as well. But, without question, it was also a warning: stay out of people's way; things work differently over here on these days.

And there were, in his vibe, also the un-asked questions – can you surf these waves well? Do you know every letter of the unwritten rulebook, and its spirit as well? Don't come crying to me if it goes wrong, he seemed to be saying: silently, invisibly, I nodded and paddled off. Ultimately, no one could escape the Rick Kane North Shore experience: no one was going to arrive into Hawaii knowing it all.

The Hawaiian Irish

For whatever reason, the Irish never really made it to Hawaii. It seemed, to me, like they cut out in California, at the furthest – at least in historical terms: but it wasn't just historical, either. This was bang up to date: even today – even in the virtual world and the long-distance-travel-is-cheap universe – the Irish didn't really seem to make it to Hawaii.

It was just too far: to many flights, and time zones, and cost; too little of the actual critical mass you need to form an Irish quorum, like you did in your average San Francisco pub. Don't get me wrong – there were Irish pubs, names, parades. There was Saint Patrick's Day, and a lot of love for Ireland, and a lot of good vibes: there just weren't that many Irish people.

Well, actually, there were one or two. Actually, only one: on an off-piste mission to Nico's, a seafood bar on the docks, a friend of a friend said to look out for a yellow and green boat that belonged to an Irishman. And, they were right: before dinner I went and found someone – a Papua New Guinean deck hand, maybe – on the deck of the *Miranda*, and asked if Trevor was home.

He emerged: white beard and all, every inch the seaman, he gave me a beer and we shot the breeze and he told sea tales – and, more, told tales of corruption and migrant workers and fishermen who spent, no joke, six months at a time on board. Even in the harbour, they couldn't come ashore: with the phlegmatism of the developing world, Trevor said, they didn't seem to mind, and made the best of whatever hand they were dealt – just like the Irish, I reckoned.

The Friday Evening Pulse

Sometimes – and yes, for sure, those were the best times – the forecast got it so, so wrong. What a triumph: no one out, or just a few of you, and the waves come through. Those were the times, for sure, when Threes felt magical and mystical: as if we were part of something a little unexplained. Under grey skies, on a Friday evening, Greg and Skipper Dave and I – and maybe a few others – watched in disbelief as the waves started to pump.

There is joy in seeing a small swell suddenly rise; seeing small waves jump to being big waves; seeing the eternal surfing hope become reality. Seeing, as well, that moment when the waves really get legitimate: seeing the ones that come though that made you pause and stop and realise that it wasn't just a once-in-the-evening freak set.

So it was one Friday evening, and the darker it got, the bigger the waves became. We stayed out late in the private playground, barely registering what was happening, and feeling the noise and the movement of the ocean change from small to medium to something else; enjoying and glorying in every moment to the full.

The Wandering Minstrels

Music sustains surfers, most of the time – and, like Ireland, ran through a lot of Hawaii: from the pub to the luau at the hotel next door to walking down the street, there would, generally, be some lilting ukulele or rock and roll melodies coming at you from some angle. Kelly's had live music – which was basically a man, or occasionally a lady, with a guitar playing in the corner each night. No frills; usually, I would end up talking to one or the other of them, given my Covid-regular status: with the musicians, I got a pretty good look, I guess, into the journeyman life of Hawaii.

Because there was that element of Hawaii, as well, I guess: I mean, why were you there? What had happened? Things hadn't worked out on the mainland, right? Or had they worked out so well that you were now just pretty much chilling out in the sun for the rest of your life? Or were you a misfit, or unlucky – or were you lucky? What was it about you that had brought you there, away from the continent that held every opportunity: did you lack ambition, love nature, or were you burned out?

Anyway, back to the music: my Dad always, always used to say that he only went to churches to hear the singing. Maybe he was telling the truth, or maybe he wasn't, but that was for sure the case for me: like some kind of Irish cartoon, I would go from music in the pub the night before to, maybe once a month, the Tongan choir in the morning.

Don't get me wrong: I hate going to churches. Hate it. Always have, unless they are empty, in which case it is ok: but the tedium and the ritual and people telling you things that may or may not be right? Empty ones, sure – the echoes, the smells, the quiet – but, otherwise, the doctrine and the regimentation and the polishing of halos and the cooped-up feeling and the unhealthiness of it all? No thanks, mate.

But, in Hawaii, you could maybe make an exception. The priests were barefoot; there were flowers everywhere. It was baking hot, so I only went for the last half an hour; the Tongan choir gave you more of a spiritual vibe than any amount of preaching.

And the people who went were worth a look, as well: this was a bit more like the real Hawaii, maybe. For sure, there was the usual quotient of tourists, like there was everywhere, but there was a lot else going on as well: those not so rich, at least at the back where I was standing. Families of Filipinos and big Samoans and Tongans and other islanders: Micronesians, and Hawaiians, and Chinese, and Japanese, and whoever else. It was, once a month, a connection with normality, and with the music of the soul, if not with higher powers.

Da Kine

It was at a guitar music night with Mike and his brothers that I really got to grips, I reckon, with one other major, major element of Hawaii: the dialect, da pidgin, the way people talked. Ho, brah.

Shoots. And, above, all, da kine: not just da kine, but da one kine – one, here, used instead of the definite or indefinite article. I guess, maybe, that someone has a linguistic term for it: imposition of the singular instead of the article, maybe, or something like that. Personally, I just thought it was pretty cool, and, I admits – admit – sometimes, when I needed to, and when it felt like the time was right – yes, for sure, sometimes, but very rarely – I even dropped it in to some conversation myself. Or tried to.

So, what I am saying is, it wasn't the car: it was da one car. It wasn't that you caught a wave; it was the one wave you caught. Mike would say to me that he took one red board out today, which pretty much said it all. It was, maybe, a way of adding emphasis. Instead of saying that is one hell of a nice surfboard, you just say the one surfboard, maybe. Either way, whatever the details, I was stoked just that I understood: that I could, a little bit, talk the talk.

Some of it, as well, was oddly Euro: not "gotten" with two d's, but gotten, for sure, with two enunciated, highlighted, emphatic t's. What was that all about? Whatever it was, for someone who had developed a little bit, maybe, of a Cali-Irish drawl after so many years in SF, it was cool: I could feel, somehow, the American accent being pushed back, tested, denied.

But nothing, nothing, prepared me for da kine: at the jam with Mike and his braddas, everything, I mean everything, was da kine. From cars to memories to trucks to boards to places to people: everyone – everything, every time and place – got called da kine. And, for sure, there is no doubt some kind of origin story: for me, what made most sense was using it in terms of the way English or Irish or Americans or Australians – or whoever – would say kind, as in 'that kind of thing'. When I thought about it like that, it made it a little easier to understand.

And, for sure, there was more: 'Ho' covered a lot of exclamations, greetings, and expressions of surprise. Bradda covered for brother – and was even better than brah, which was, even to the locals, sort of a cliché. And there were cool Hawaiian phrases, as well: E komo mai, 'amakua, pau hana, wahine, and a lot of other surfy- or ocean-related expressions. For some reason, as well, there was also the way the Hawaiians said the word "already": it was everywhere: come on already, finished already, tired already, time to surf – already.

The jewel in the crown, though – and the way to sniff out a local – was 'shoots'. So, so cool. Shoot: I got it wrong. But, shoots: ok, that is cool. Wow. What a landmine: no question, if you used shoots like you were using shoot, you weren't, maybe, quite as in touch with the vibe that you maybe thought you were. By reading Chas Smith I got to grips with it before I made any bad mistakes in front of Zach and Chuck: Smith, like me, couldn't figure out where it had come from – and maybe even got its use wrong a few times – but never, ever, ever used it instead of 'shoot'.

There were a couple of other things, maybe, that also helped: the way that Ireland as well, lived – big time – by underground slang. Where did it come from? Some of it was cockney, some of it was Gaelic, and some of it, for sure, was just deep, deep Irish code, that could only make sense to the locals. Get up the yard? Get up out of that? Get out of that garden? Good luck with those ones, tourists and arrivistes. And one thing I thought was cool, and also totally Irish, was that the Hawaiians also stayed clear, whenever they could, of the more hostile expletives: In Ireland, 'feck' was considered pretty harmless – but, at the same time, still sort of getting your point across.

In Hawaii, it was the same sort of thing: 'you fock, you focker, dat focker': they all covered what people were trying to say without, maybe, coming across as super directly confrontational: they could be intense words, for sure, but maybe to be taken with just a pinch of salt, sometimes. Anything to sidestep authority, right?

Maybe that was why it felt good to be there: maybe that is why I felt more at home there than I ever did in San Francisco, despite the fact that Hawaii was geographically further away: maybe, like Andy Martin, I was a born islander – albeit from a cold one – and understood the way style ,and karma, and even repartee, worked on islands as opposed to mainlands.

Technique

No doubt, my surfing changed – things smoothed out. Zach saw to that, that was for sure: rarely did a day go by when he didn't have some kind of gripe about my, or someone else's, style. Occasionally it would get annoying, and some people just laughed at him: I tried to avoid being a blind acolyte, because he could be hyper critical – but occasionally, I admit, wrote down a few notes here and there.

Everything was analysed, broken down, excoriated by him: stance and board and pop and everything in between. From smoothing out styles to bottom turning in new ways to fades to using hips: at the start, Zach had called me 'The Mummy' because of the way my arms hung out in front of me.

And, gradually, listening to the other surfers and watching the surf cam rewinds, things began to change. Moves began to smooth out: I started to move even more in line with the flow and shape of the wave: hanging in the pocket, and generating speed, and making it around sections. Going high and hand jiving and pumping and occasionally just standing there; lapsing in to a lean-back and blowing a kiss to the passing tourist boats, if I felt like it.

But the best, the icing in the cake, was getting prone-outs dialled: Zach, after a while – after working on pretty much everything else – zoomed in on my prone outs. Now, I agree: after a lifetime of beach breaks and closeouts and complex Irish waves, the prone out had never been a big priority. Kick-outs were more fun – but here, in Hawaii, it was an aesthetic necessity: an element of style, a way of signing out of the wave in style, with this flourish of accomplishment.

And so I worked on it: worked on the timing, and straightening my back leg, and positioning and pivoting my front foot, and all of that. Worked and worked until I had it dialled: until I was ready, seeing Zach paddle out late in the evening, to shout over to him, telling him to watch. Already, this had embarrassed him, which was sort of the point, but the best was yet to come: paddling back out, I called to him, across the line up, asking if he had seen it. 'Did you see that?" I asked, to his horror. 'Don't do that", he said, as I paddled closer. 'You are not twelve years old. Only twelve-year-olds ask if people have seen their waves". But he was rattled, and I laughed, and things got back in to balance.

Night Surf (No Leash)

At Paradise, on some days, bombers came through. I saw Chuck sitting way, way, out a couple of times – one man in the middle of the ocean sort of thing, and what seemed like a football pitch away – and was baffled by his thinking. It all came together, though, when the bombers rolled through, and he rode them all the way to the inside in a way that almost defied physics. Why; how? The wave often looked like it wouldn't have the legs – but would then hit some other contour and almost reform, and continue to peel, and offer a big and wide-open face for whoever wanted it.

It was different take-off to Three's, because it was a less perfect wave, maybe – and could easily, easily catch you out. But, on its day, when things came together, it was a big wall, and a beautiful sight and, best of all, a secret spot in plain sight: the reports and the cams overlooked it, and no one really surfed there, despite how amazingly good it was. Hey, if there wasn't a report on it, it didn't exist – right?

It was also the place where I lost my board: talk about traumatic. Just a couple of weeks before the end of the year – what a year – and all seemed well: a routine late evening surf at Paradise, easy, no need even for a leash – a nice way to end the year, sort of a series of victory rolls, of chill times with the pressure off. The waves rolled through, and I hooked a few, and a few more, and went left to end the evening, and – boom – no board.

Not a whisper, not a hint: nothing. Gone, vaporised, into the ether: the more I swam and looked, the more it wasn't there. Obscured, maybe, by the lights of Waikiki, or blown by the trades, or captured by the current: eventually, I hit that inflection point when I knew I had to abandon ship, call off the search, and swim in.

It never, ever reappeared: I searched the tide lines, put up signs, left messages at the surf shops. Waited until two in the morning, when the tide had come in, and walked the beach again, to Kaisers and back: put ads online, and even offered a reward: called it into the Coast Guard – they liked it when people did that, in case they found a lost board and started worrying about who may have been attached to it – and let the beach boys, and Chuck, and Zach, and everyone, know. But, unlike others, mine ever turned up again. I was totally upset, and I loved that board – but, yeah, it was a only a board.

Rewind II: Pre-Covid Ireland

Tom Crean's statue, Annascaul

Cold Start

After leaving San Francisco, but before starting Hawaii, there was another stage: home. But what was the reality: what was Ireland like to tap back in to after so long in California? Like anywhere, maybe, for a returning native – but a little bit trickier, as well: a little bit more ethereal, a little bit more mystique. It wasn't the place I had left behind many years before, that was for sure – and I had always, on trips home, hit the road to California again: there was too much fun in the sun to be had; too much of newness and thrills and spills and adventure and misadventure and late nights and Golden State sunset surfs and all the rest. But, for whatever reason, Ireland persisted: the one place, maybe, that could still be called home, even after twenty years away.

That was a threshold, for sure: the way I figured it, if you hadn't tried to dial in to Ireland after that twenty-year mark, it was unlikely that you were going to do it. Ten years, no problem – but after twenty, I don't know: you are sort of pushing the boundaries of re-integration, right?

But maybe I was sort of thinking that surfing could help: surfing, the seemingly eternal passport that would make you feel at home anywhere in the world that had rideable waves, a local crew, and some wax. Right? Wasn't that what it was about – a passport to exotic locales, in communion with like-minded cruisers? A tool that would crack any country with a coastline; something that, at a spiritual level, would bear you through cultures and societies and economies and drop you of at the nearest pointbreak? After that, for sure, you were on your own – but it was, always, a start.

So maybe surfing could crack Ireland open again; maybe it would find a chink in the Emerald Isle's armour of time; maybe it would let me go home. Maybe it would set me up with enough stoke to open other doors; maybe Eire would be open to seeing what I could bring back from the rest of the world. Maybe surfing would let me back in to Ireland – but, before even that, I had to figure out a way to get back in to surfing in Ireland in the first place.

After all that time, there were, apparently, going to be a few catches: first, it wasn't going to happen overnight. Over a few years, sure, maybe: but not in the short term. Second, it wasn't going to happen in a linear way: though I may have prised the door open, apparently the surf-travel-life paradigm hadn't let the sun set on it just yet. There might be years, still, in Hawaii. But, I reckoned, I had to make a start.

The local beach break was the obvious place: from there, nods from semi-remembered faces and dreams of missions west. In the old days, it was just one long party: this was, no joke, the kind of thing that happened: in a country town, some chancers, aged maybe twelve or something, we standing in the side of the road spraying cars with water pistols, just for a laugh – just the way I would have done. Loving it, and winning, and dominating events, until the surfers came by – loving it, until OMA turned to the Masochist and asked him if he just saw that – if he just saw the water pistol spray hitting his car?

The Masochist confirmed that he had, and after that it was action stations – a bottle of water was dug out from beneath boards and wetsuits, a quick u-turn, and.... boom! The young lads got it back with interest a direct hit with a litre or so of water. You should have seen their faces: the biter bit, the shock, the karma vibe. And the surfmobile, u-turning again to get back on track, was breaking apart with laughter and hoots. "Drencher!" said the Masochist.

All that, too, for better or for worse, would have changed: far from the wild revelries that look on waves as an afterthought, these new school trips, I was hearing, would consist of early starts and same-day cross-country missions and double surfs and peak nutrition and little, if any, alcohol: these trips would be like clean, tight commando strikes; the new missions west would resemble military operations more than circuses. Hey, that was ok: I could live with that, as long as I hooked a few.

Dawn Patrols

For sure, each mission was different, but each had its own commonalities: the text or call or beachside discussion a few days before; the rumours of a swell. The zeroing-in about which days we could get away, and which spot to hit: an eye on the weather – an eye on personal commitments, and basically looking for any way out of them. And the narrowing down further, the day before: the confirmation of the mission (unless things changed overnight); the fixing of dings; the packing and drying of wetsuits. The trying-not-to-forget-the-essentials part: what to bring, like hats and gloves in winter, vying against the need and drive to be streamlined, minimalist, low-maintenance.

The night before always had its own sub-dynamics: the futile attempt to go to bed early, the negotiations about departure times: with Newstalk, the eventual compromise – like it always was – on a pre-dawn take off time. And the moments of slight fear just before turning out the light, echoing from early surf trip days and competing with the stoke and escapism at what was to come: and the four, or five, or six hours of rest.

And the getting up: the moving quietly, and the shower, and the tea; the moving of boards and gear outside to await the driver. The need, for sure, not to hold anyone up: it wasn't quite the formula one pit stop scene, but that early in the morning in the pitch black, it could sometimes feel like that. The under-ten-minutes loading target: the kind help with the gear while I went back in to lock up and maybe finish the cup of tea. Get in; adjust the car seat; double check the racks: buckle up, last checks, and.... Go.

And then the road: the darkness, and streetlights, and dawn patrol trucks. The milk vans and newspaper deliveries and the birds in the trees and the empty villages: all the while, getting up to speed, getting comfortable, shooting the breeze with the driver, feeling the gradual increase in stoke. And on to the main roads, out of the villages: the surprising busyness of it all, even at that hour; the concern for the future of civilisation – all those people driving so fast, so early. What was pushing them, or pulling them? Where was everyone going? I mean, they couldn't all be surfing, right?

And, gradually, the open road: the city rush giving way to narrower highways and fewer cars: the darkness persisting, and the weather changing in bands of rain or fog or starry skies. The re-checking of forecasts and destinations – sometimes, rarely, the last-minute changes of course, and all the debate and edginess that went with it. The jokes, the music, the news on Newstalk's radio: the phone calls with Mossy or Eoin or Foamo, or another regional point man: above all, laced through it all, the anticipation, the stoke, and – occasionally – the fear.

Things never really got groovy, though, until about halfway through. Maybe at Carrick-on Shannon, or whatever the halfway point was: the warm petrol station; the hot sambos, and the extra supplies that the passenger had learned by bitter experience to bring (you may not get a chance to eat again for a while, buddy, depending on how the day went). And back in the car, and heat back on, and yeah baby: another cup of tea and a slab of Dairy Milk and a hot ham and cheese – and past the halfway point, and across the Shannon, and things starting to get bright, literally: and the feeling creeping up on you that you were styling.

And the moment: the place where and when – on the Sligo road, anyway – things suddenly opened up, and you knew you were in the west. The sudden view of the road winding between big, green hills: the brightening sky behind them, and the deep, deep vibe of freedom that every surf mission brings.

But then things change again: back to business; a hint of fear; checking signs and weather: looking for the glimpse of swell along the coast. Making calls about which back road to take, which spots to check: fine-tuning the mission as the road starts to get smaller again, and as the traffic arteries turn back in to capillaries – until, finally, on a single lane track leading to the coast, you are right back where you began, just on the other side of the country. And the blast of cold air as you step out: the first look, the moment of judgement: and the certain knowledge that either you have scored, or will score later in the day, or that you are looking at a long, long drive home.

Bohs, Dohs

Never go back, they say in the books, and in the movies – and in the parables, and in the fables. Never try to re-create the old days: never expect things to be the same. Whatever it was, it was a time and a place; it was a period of life, an era, an epoch, a moment in time. Memories should be treasured, and not reenacted; events should be written about with misty eyes and rose tints – not grappled with in person. Any such attempt will, at best, fail elegantly – at worst, lead to embarrassment, injury, humiliation.

But this time there was no choice: closing in on twenty years in the US, thoughts had turned more and more to Ireland. To Eireann's green fields – which actually do exist, which are not just in songs – and the lack of fear-inducing headline news; to stone walls and muddy tracks; to the cold and the rain and the dark; to the wind and the sun and the sky. To reflections on empty waves and good vibes: to the glory days of early surf adventure with close mates or whoever happened to be around.

But so many roads back into Ireland, metaphorically, had been blocked: I mean the twenty-years-of-conventionality-versus-twenty-years-of-adventure roadblocks – the expectations and the minor cultural differences that could too easily offend: a vague Americanisation, that was occasionally at odds with the essence of Irish culture. No entry, read the imagined signs: but would the same apply to the waves? Or, as always, would surfing be different – would surfing be the key?

At 6:30 a.m., *ish*, on a winter's day, it was time to find out. Leaving home in the dark, three hours later a rare gleam of sun greeted Newstalk and I after the habitual cross-country mission: average waves at the lefthander, and a crowd at the right, held little appeal to the driver. (For better or for worse, after a long time away I didn't have much say about where we went, just nodding quietly in assent as he suggested we try somewhere out-of-the-way. I could have had no idea at the time that that was the key

– that that was the ticket to adventure and integration. Because amongst all the locals, all the surfers, not everyone wanted to veer off the beaten path. Those who did – and who could keep quiet about it, and not do stupid things like write books – got invited back.)

And so we changed and hiked over rocks, across a river, and around the headland – dodging cows and broken-down barbed wire fences as we went, en route to a quiet bay. There, we paddled out to a right-hander that was hosting just one surfer, and he didn't seem too concerned about being sheeped. In the glistening morning sun, we forgot the cold, and the slippy rocks, and the long drive: now, there was just the raw energy and clean-ness and wide-open spaces of the North Atlantic to contend with once again.

That, in itself, took energy to process: muscle memory echoed of fear and adrenalin as sets lumbered beneath our dangling feet. Eventually, one came that looked right: on an ancient single fin – another relic from the early days – I took off and saw deepest blue combined with sunlight: saw Newstalk on the shoulder, and green hills in the distance, and the rush of water up the face. Maybe, I reckoned, the door to Ireland had, just fractionally, opened.

Wanting to document the moment, I asked the third man – the soul surfer – what the place was called. It seemed natural for it to have no name: but he told me it was called Bohs, for no apparent reason. Was it the Irish for cow? Was it short for bohemian – was it "bows", a reference to the arc of the wave? Who knew – Newstalk stubbornly called it "Dohs" ever afterwards, so maybe I misheard. It was too soon after returning to claim naming rights, that was for sure, so I just went with the flow.

White Rocking

It is probably, to be honest, one of the least best waves around. Not just on the East Coast, and not just in Ireland, but globally: but White Rock, for sure, was having its lockdown day in the sun. A last-resort sort of place that would pick up tiny bumps of wind swell before abruptly closing out, it was in stark contrast with its belligerent neighbour in K-Bay. But now, there was – no joke – up to maybe seventy surfers in in the small surf zone, fanatically tracking the times of the low tide. And darkness was a threat in winter; and the cold was an issue: but, more than that, there was the threat of the crowd to the crowd: boards flying left and right, and the continual risk of head trauma.

One thing about being an Irish surfer, though: you have to be, all the time, relentlessly inventive. You have to find waves, and concoct surfing, wherever you can: you had to almost imagine it in to being good. And I am, for sure, being too harsh: the wave, or what there was of it, saved us many times. Saved us from repetition and boredom, thanks to its own variety: As the tide changed, so did the wave. From mellow rights on the dead low to a peak favouring more rights, and occasional lefts, as it rose; to wally lefts at the very north end just before the wave closed up shop, and was drowned by high water. (The latter were precariously close to the rocks, but, because everyone had gotten their eye in by that stage, no one seemed to mind.)

And there was a magic to it, I guess: a uniqueness, a changing of the guard, a literal new wave of surfers and new people, Covid-spooked, tuning in to the outdoors. For many, it wouldn't last, and White Rock would go back to being its old self – but for a while there it was, no question, the place to be: a hidden corner of the dirty old town's coastline, not all that easily accessible. Amidst affluent surrounds, the workingman's game of surfing comes to town and crashes the party: amidst backdrops of cliffs and an island and old houses, black-clad figures on the peripheries of polite society gathered. A small, narrow window into the surfing universe; a portal to other places and experiences.

Kerry

Some missions embrace you, some missions school you. Some surf trips will light your fire, others will rain on your parade; not every aspect of surfing was a welcome home; not every mission opened new doors. Not every trip was a good example – some were terrible warnings, and, as I stood by a bathtub filled with an unknown and viscous green liquid in a freezing garage, at first light, in a town on the Kerry – Limerick border, and thought of other places, and other people, I knew it was my time: this was a good moment, I reckoned, to see if one could roll with the considerable punches that Ireland could impose.

On the road with Newstalk, it started with a puncture and a hobble to a garage early in the morning; once the wheel was changed, the mission felt like it has been somehow jinxed. You know that sort of feeling? We were running late: it was already a ten-hour round trip – and the tide, waiting for no man, sure wasn't going to wait for you; there was no real margin for error. Technically, we should probably have turned around and gone home. Of course, there was no way we were doing that.

On a surf trip – more than anywhere – there is no turning back, so we kept driving. Over the rolling hills of Kerry, towards Tom Crean's home – past Inch, along the winding coat road to Anascaul and the North Pole Pub. Towards the statue of Crean and the puppies in the Antarctic: past, also, giant onshore waves that were in no way surfable. Just then, it was tough to gauge the mood of that surf trip: I was feeling a bit edgy over a lady in San Francisco; it was February, always the nadir of the Irish year. But, we were in Kerry, propelled by the endless optimism of the surfer – always believing that the next great wave lay right around the corner.

Eventually arriving at a sheltered bay, the familiar black dots in the water – distant wetsuits, floating on invisible boards – made us feel like, maybe, there would be some surf. More concerned with the waves than the people, there seemed potential: an occasional right hander, rolling around the bay in the winter sunlight. But, yeah, definitely, we knew we had missed the tide; knew it wasn't going to work out: there was a sixth sense of predestination, amplified by the car door flying open and over-extending in a gust of wind, that we pretty much just ignored.

All hope wasn't lost, though: this was Ireland, and something always happens. Always. On this occasion, a New Zealander roaming the coast in his pick-up truck: after the usual roadside chat, he told me – noting that I had been left behind by the other surfers and was dragging my feet – to hop on the back. Grabbing my board and safely encased in my wetsuit, we overtook the advance party – first to reach the beach, I achieved the all-important surf privilege of being the first to paddle out.

The waves were evasive, except for one: on the wrong board, and with freezing, freezing feet, I hooked a super windy right and weaved to the shore. The backdrop – of rolling cliffs and harsh Irish winter sunlight – was spectacular. Soon after, we packed up and drove home: a lot of resources, and time, and attention; a lot of tiredness, bordering on paranoia. A lot of miles covered: not much to show for it, but sometimes you have to pay the piper. Sometimes Ireland demands more than it gives back; sometimes it will test you.

Bad Times at the Point

Maybe it was guilt: after all, none of us were really meant to be there. By the letter of the law we were ok, barely, but it didn't save us from the keen eye of West of Ireland local society – or from ourselves. But everyone needed escapes from lockdowns, no matter how doctrinaire you are, and the ocean seemed pretty safe: at the best of times, surfers always kept their distance from each other, and more so then ever now.

There was still an odd, almost childish vibe, though, when Newstalk and I met Mossy by the point. We had gotten up way, way before dawn – Carrick-on-Shannon, the halfway petrol station stop, was pretty much the first time we saw daylight – and had sort of half expected to be there by ourselves. Not to be: more than one familiar face caught our eyes from across the grey and windy car park. We were torn between being polite; flat out pretending that we hadn't seen them; or, even more fantastically, believing that we weren't actually there ourselves.

Whatever about the guilt – it was time to surf. Scoping the line up from the sucky, rocky ledge, things seemed promising: the crowd had filled in, but there were still different sections of the wave offering different rides. Life was good: things were easy, once we got in the water – surfing was all right, after all, and not a mortal sin. There were smiles and nods and repartee and reeling right handers: at lunch, we had only good waves, and good vibes, to look back on.

After that – as they do in surfing – things changed. One moment you're cruising, next moment you're nothing: I was barely a blip on the metaphysical radar as I saw the swell build, saw the crowd fill in and felt tiredness approaching: felt the wrong-board feeling, felt cold, and felt whatever other contextual or circumstantial excuses sprang to mind. The Guru, sitting beside me, reckoned the same thing: "No rhythm", he said.

The waves, though, were bombing. Guys on big boards were dropping straight in to barrels as the take off deepened and ledged until it was only the bravest, fastest, and best taking off in the spots I usually liked to try to hog. Scratching for a few, I took the wrong ones, and got washed around a bit, just to complete my sense that it wasn't going to be my afternoon.

I was reassured that the lads weren't necessarily scoring either: Mossy seemed to have too small a board, and was doing his sit-halfway-down-the-point thing, and Newstalk was always a mystery: often happy to sit and chill and float and chat, he would, occasionally, pull something out of the hat that forced a total reassessment of his whole vibe. This was that day: towards early evening – or late afternoon, in winter Ireland – I saw him bearing down on me on what can only be described as a millennium wave: big and glassy and grey-shimmering; blue board and good positioning and black wetsuit, and everyone getting out of the way.

Sickened, I tried to look away, or at least hope that I hadn't been seen gawking from the shoulder. There was a method to it: nothing good could come of a journey home with an elated companion when things hadn't worked out so well personally. At least, that was my thinking: but, seriously, I can't imagine any other surfer feeling differently, if they are honest with themselves.

It was way after dark, later, and we had just stopped for some roadside bladder control down a grassy lane, Irish style, when the subject finally came up. I can't even remember who mentioned it: maybe it was me who eventually had to casually ask if he got any good ones, just to get it out of the way. It would have looked strange if I hadn't enquired, I suppose. Anyway, whatever happened, that is when the floodgates opened: for at least an hour, I was treated to a description of every aspect of the wave. At times it felt like he was probing to see if I really hadn't seen it; at times I felt guilty about maintaining that I wasn't sure: that I might have seen it; that I didn't think it was him; that I was too focused on my own world; or whatever sprang to mind.

Eventually, months later, I confessed: yes, for sure, we were grown men but every so often aspects of the schoolyard would creep in. I told him, at an appropriate moment – at a time when things were going well enough for me that I could go down that particular road – that I had seen the wave: admitted that, overlaid with my dodgy afternoon session, it would have been too much to stomach to admit that I had seen him in a moment of serious, serious glory. He just laughed and nodded and laughed again: who knows, maybe it had been a double bluff, and he had known all along that I had watched it.

Unleashed at Lisadell

We had bypassed Easkey, which already had sort of annoyed me, but what could I do? Passengers don't decide, baby – and if I wanted to take a look in and say hi to local acquaintances, or have a post-session pint in McGowans, it wasn't going to happen on this mission. The lads laughed; they knew the score. Their mindset, maybe, was a little more focused: get the waves and go home. Selfishly, after being away for so long I wanted more: the chance to soak in the Wild West; build some connections; re-live past glories.

So I sulked in the back, but when we got to Lisadell – a lesser wave, on the other side of town – things looked up: big lefts peeled through the crowd, and we were all likely to get our share.

It wasn't the easiest wave in the world, that was for sure, but the tide and the vibe was right, and the waves spun down the point.

But nothing was like Easkey: heading to Grange after the first session, what would have been a lunchtime glass of Guinness and local pub repartee turned in to a furtive can of roadside cheap beer in the drizzle. Less than inspiring, not quite the *dolce vita*, but we ate and laughed and talked about our rides – and that was pretty much enough: after that, taking in an obscure wave at a ruined Abbey on the way, it was time to surf again.

By then, things had hotted up a bit: more panel vans had appeared. Even though it was for sure a B-class set up, it had its days and acolytes and devotees and locals; faces that seemed half-familiar from other waves appeared out of the woodwork and the green fields and the stone walls.

The paddle out wasn't easy, but was harder at low tide: it was bottoming out on that post-lunch session, and, somehow – like so often happens – I just wasn't feeling it the same way as I had been in the morning. Something had gone of kilter, and on my second wave I took off too deep. Instantaneously, my leash twanged beneath the water, and I felt the sinking feeling of a weightless ankle as my board surfed itself to shore. The swim in; the dinged board; the end of the session: reviewing it all on the grassy slopes – on the narrow winding West of Ireland backroad roadside: the long drive home, and – already – the preparing to return.

Dutchies

The tensions I was to discover in Hawaii weren't totally absent in Ireland, either. Thigs cut both ways: if at times Hawaii would feel Irish, so too could the reverse hold. Changing on a patch of bog by a wave called Dutchman's, Mossy and Newstalk and I felt the edge in the form of a big blue tractor: an angry farmer, later identified as one John, could not, in any way, have been more offended at our presence. Could not have been angrier, or less welcoming, or more aggressive: did all but kick us out on whatever premise of access he felt he had: shook his pitchfork, and turned red, and glared, and shouted. Our cars, he warned us, could easily end up in the water one day.

He stormed off and began – equally angrily – to belligerently shovel some seaweed from one patch to another, as if to prove his point. The scene was so real, but also tinged with such pathos, that the lads were caught between laughing and crying. For me, I felt the usual sense of shock when such outbursts occurred: an echo in my stomach that lasted through an indifferent session.

But it was a session when Mossy got a bomber on his backside, so close in front of me that I could see his feet in mid-air as he popped and set himself up – could see a wry smile on his face as if he knew it was going to be a good ride – things altered, fractionally. The farmer faded in to the haze of the ocean and the cliffs and the sea spray; the final memories were purged, like everything always was, in the ocean spray.

The Beach Bar, Aughris

On a summer's night, we surfed until it was almost too late to eat or drink. At Easkey right, it had been the classic situation: the most demanding waves, when one is least prepared for them. Fresh from a cross-country journey, and into the relative cold, and into the big bad world: from the protected warmth of the car, into the elements. From security to bravado: from comfort to its apogee. Fortunately, we had put in the orders for food in earlier on over at the Aughris Beach Bar, and there was always the chance of a quiet pint if you asked politely.

The locals at the bar had the usual mixed vibe towards surfers: Mossy looked like a Guard, an Irish policeman, and was constantly being mistaken for one. I had no idea why everyone thought he was a law enforcer: maybe it was the build, or maybe he somehow resembled some kind of image of what Irish people thought the police should, or did, look like. He told me he got it all the time; the local boozers never really relaxed; we ate and laughed; outside, small waves broke in the cove.

The next day, we cruised to Enniscrone via Easkey, taking whatever waves came our way en route. There were moments of reflection over a pint in the Enniscrone Hotel; the usual confidences and reservations swapped between surfers on every trip. As always, some elements were found to be in common, others less so: it didn't matter, really, as we jumped in at the left again with an element of schoolboy recklessness. The waves were good, and glassy, though the loss of reflexes over lunchtime pints could be felt.

The booze, no doubt, caused some of the bravado – but also resulted in a few twinges: back in Aughris, we stretched and chatted and felt old wounds acting up again. Sitting in the room, we realised that maybe we weren't as young as we used to be, but that that was still sort of ok: the basics were still in place. We could still surf, and reckoned that, if we were lucky, we would for a while. Not only that, but we had our gear more dialled in than ever: we knew, also, spots and conditions – and were, probably, better surfers than we used to be.

As the night grew late, we laughed at the old school escapades when midnight was just the starting point: this time, even though we hadn't planned to do the dawn patrol the next day, we still probably wrapped it up by around one. I strolled out for one last look at the waves in the Irish moonlight: in this new scene characterised by so much that was different, that was another thing that wasn't like to change any time soon.

The Monastery

When Newstalk told me that he intended – ruthlessly, mercilessly, to get me back into the groove of Ireland – in every way, every day, from current affairs to geography to society to whatever else – he wasn't joking. At a pre-dawn petrol station on the Republic – Northern Ireland border, I realised that Ireland still had many faces, many sides, and that disputed borders and territories was still one of them. Near Enniskillen, we ducked across the border into the black north, moving from tricolours to union jacks in the blink of a sleepy eye.

The border was porous, but the difference in tone was tangible: in the old days, the roads in the north used to be oh-so-superior to those in the republic border counties: now, the north seemed a place of neglect – a forgotten colony, its erstwhile shipbuilding might no longer of great interest to its colonial masters. Pot-holed roads, run down vibes, a general sense of pessimism and abandonment, all in contrast to the exuberance of the south – and there was, no matter what anyone says, still an edge: still ruins of surveillance posts, and elements of planning and society that resonated of the martial; of fear; of divides.

The traffic was bad, so we had plenty of time to look around before emerging back into the republic at a border village best known for low-stakes gambles on petrol prices – euros or sterling, depending on the exchange rate. The lasses in the breakfast area were friendly, though, as we cruised through Letterkenny into an alien, lunar Donegal landscape: between the rain and the hail, the journey came to life again.

Eventually, after winding roads through offbeat villages, we peeled off into a monastery: Newstalk told me that the wave behind it was so good that, if he won the lottery, he was going to buy the land and kick all the monks off – just so he could surf it himself. In the deserted parking lot, I couldn't see many members of the clergy to persecute – but, going inside to see if there was a cup of tea around (there wasn't), I was welcomed by warmth, and – though I am careful about saying it – a tangible spiritual vibe.

The go, at the Monastery, was not even to check it: get changed, walk, and don't forget to bring a change and food and whatever else. The hike along the inlet was too long for reccys – the forest too deep, the weather too cold. Plus, what did I know, anyway? It was the same story: keep my mouth shut, my eyes open: don't bother making too many creative suggestions to the veterans, just watch and learn the protocol and approach.

Eventually, the inlet appeared: in the middle, across what I guess was a river mouth shoal, a left was just starting to show. Living in fear of the tide – and with, maybe, a little steam to let off after the five-hour drive – Newstalk was out there before I was even in my wetsuit. The mornings were always tough: even after driving across the country, I often felt as if I was still waking up. Not wanting to antagonise, but not keen on the hustle either, I bided my time, and stretched, and wandered the yellow sands before following in his wake.

At first, the wave, when I got out there, seemed too fast: too racy and violent and unmakeable, especially on my backhand. I hooked a few, and began to run the numbers: a day of exhaustion, and the preparations the night before: the prospect of double exhaustion the next day, all for some semi-closeouts in the middle of nowhere. "Chill out", Newstalk said, detecting my vibe. 'It will come".

Gradually, almost mythically, it did: with the changing tide, shoulders appeared along the racetrack, and the wave became makeable; steel-black and gun-metal-grey under dark skies, the river mouth began to work. With it, locals appeared – but they seemed friendly enough: in North Donegal's former bandit country, a different kind of etiquette prevailed, in which neighbours were treated with as much caution as strangers. There had been too much hostility in these parts already; pretty much everyone had had their fill of bad vibes over the years. That kind of washed-out approach meant that no one really got vibed up there, as far as I could sense.

Bearing a bizarre similarity to Elands, a left point in South Africa and scene of some glory days in the past, the waves reared and backed off and walled up: for an hour, or maybe two, conditions came together. I watched a rotund surfer on a tiny board pick off some sets; watched Newstalk showcase his familiarity – and watched where he sat, took off, and paddled back out. Between the ethereal vibe of the place, and the waves, it was as close to surf-transcendence as it was ever possible to get.

And that was it: back on shore; lock and load; book it home. Exhilarated as we were by the waves, the pendulum battle between exhaustion and adrenaline went back and forth, as it always did: episodes of sleep ending abruptly when I would get asked, pointedly and loudly, what I thought about Brexit, or

Sinn Fein, or the new housing regulations, or whatever. I knew, though, that in Ireland a wingman had jobs to do as well – one of them being to keep the driver awake, and also act as a quasi-navigator, safety officer, Mars-bar unwrapper, coffee-cup holder, water-bottle unscrewer, sounding board, and the rest.

The other reality – one that no one could ever deny – was that I would never, ever, have gotten there myself. Never, buddy. Averse to driving, and to early mornings, and leaving home after already being away so much, I was, though surfing and mates, being exposed to bizarre hidden corners of the island, making a small country seem both accessible and vast. And there was – like there always is in surfing – that element of secret advantages: a cabal, a sect, a traveling covert op to tap the source.

The Quantum Flux

Every surf spot has its lore; some more than others. In some places – and this for sure, was one – even the spelling of the name was inconsistent: suggestive of secrecy, of age, of evasiveness. I mean, how could you find a surf spot if you couldn't even spell it, right? Sometimes, driving, you could even picture the local hardy bucks in the county council having a laugh as they entitled each road sign differently, in true rural Irish comedic style – but there seemed to be more to it than that: this was the kind of place that didn't necessarily want to be found, or discovered, any more than it already had been. The various handles also suggested a wish for discretion, for privacy: for flying under the radar.

To compound these mysteries, the place itself was rarely discussed amongst Irish surfers. Whether this was because of secretiveness, inaccessibility, or the very fickle nature of the break, I never really figured out: I had only, until the mission, had a hazy memory of an older surfer, many years before, telling me that it was the best wave in Ireland, on its day. And I had, as well, a hazy image of a picture I had seen of a bizarre J-Bay-looking set up with super bizarrely-located mountains nearby – trippy, surreal, and (I reckoned) possibly just invented.

I also had no idea where to start: having been in exile for many years, the niceties of tide, swell, swell period, swell size, swell direction, wind strength and direction, and broader weather conditions – not to mention time of year – were all way, way beyond me. Fortunately, I had been taken into the inner circle of Newstalk and Mossy, both of whom had the place dialled. I wasn't quite sworn to secrecy – but, no doubt, discretion was advised. Big, big time.

More broadly, things had been, at best, so-so in the lead-up to the mission. After a series of hit and miss trips, culminating in that epic drive to Kerry which had been punctuated by a punctured tire and resulted in only one wave – a long way to go for a few seconds of glory –faith in the Irish surf paradigm was under threat. It felt, to be totally honest, too complex: too unreliable, too cold, too harsh; independently, the Irish winter had also taken its toll after so many years in the sun.

With all that as a backdrop, Mossy and I arrived late to an irate B&B owner in a far-flung town – far out, bust still nowhere near the mythical, mysto break – which, fortunately or unfortunately, also happened to be the local party zone. The cold was cutting; we strolled the wet streets looking for a late bag of chips amidst intensely biting spells of sleet. The only option, to our minds, was to go inside: not back to the B&B, necessarily, but to a selection of the finest pubs we could find. There, we sat by fires talking to locals; exchanged surf and travel stories; felt the pre-Covid (by, maybe, a month) energy of jammed, jointed, packed-to-the rafters back rooms dripping with musical heritage that are the DNA of so many country locales; and listened to whoever was on stage for the evening's jam.

Some of the winter melted away in such places, that was for sure, though it was right there waiting for us outside the door. Back in the B&B, sleep didn't come easily, for whatever reasons: by the time the morning rolled around, the effects of the accumulated winter; the trip; the night before; and tiredness all hit home. Even an ancient spiritual monument, shining in the morning sun, couldn't alleviate the anomie: as I waited outside a petrol station while Mossy built a breakfast roll, the whole point of surfing seemed to fade in to the ether.

After a little bit of a drive, we still weren't out of the woods yet: not knowing the break, I could only study Mossy's face as we parked and examined the line-up. There were clean lines, but one passing surfer suggested we might, maybe, have arrived too late – surely one of the most fatal sentences a surfer can be dealt. We both knew the costs of the extra pint the night before, and had each paid it on prior trips: we could only hope that the same penalty wouldn't have to be paid today.

Still, Mossy looked tense. I couldn't figure him out, at that moment in time, but was definitely not getting my hopes up. Buying ourselves some time, we drove around the headland and a long way down another road to another, trickier break: again, the swell was there; the weather was there; but the wave wasn't on. In partial dejection, we retreated back to where we had first parked – back to square one and with nowhere to hide, gazing out to sea. We stared hard, willing the swell to come up: it didn't; we waited some more; we decided to get in anyway.

Even that wasn't easy: Mossy had the walk-out dialled, picking his way across the patches of bog and rocky headland paths with agility and style: he was in the lineup and surfing while I was, cursing, dropping in to bog holes and using the nose of my board to lever myself out. Finally, after a hell walk, I was at the rocks on the shore: there were still no waves to speak of.

With no other options to dream up, there was nothing to do but paddle out: nothing to do but shoot the breeze with a longboarder who was, I am pretty sure, wearing webbed gloves. I think I remember that because, when the first hint – the first distant, distant rumbling of life – like an echo on the horizon, like a glimmer of light; like the green flash of a sunset – chimerically appeared, he didn't paddle for it. Instead, he held up his webbed hands, as if to sort of say "All yours, I am not a predator", or something – and I hooked it on his inside.

And yes, for sure, things got better: better, better, better. Surreally better, as the groundswell finally decided to arrive and swept, quietly but increasingly majestically, around the point. I got a few, and a few more, and at a certain corner of the wave, I can tell you, and even though it sounds melodramatic, another corner was reached. Life could nail you – but how could it be bad, how could it be bad at all, when nature could offer us such sights?

Here is what happened: the swell had grown, and, taking off outside, the wave let you in nice and easy. Approaching halfway, though, there wasn't so much of a step in the face as a kink in the reef – a place where the wave changed shape, and speeded up, and sort of hooked, and maybe even changed colour. And so the green, glassy wall stood up, and the most delicate, delicate trim was required not to upset or race it: instead, almost no movement was required to stay in the pocket.

That was, pretty much, what happened – except for something else. That was it, in conventional terms – but what about the way the board clicked in to the shape of the wave at that moment, as if it had been waiting for that split second for ever – and what about the way that, because it did that, I was blown sway, standing there, by a sense of the universe falling in to place – of synchronicity, and cosmic forces, and by the total profoundness, probably more profound than anything else in this book, of that one second in time? Everything, for once, changed: a quantum flux; a fleeting, momentary through-the-looking-glass moment where the past was swept away and the future opened out.

As we surfed, the tide changed, and things got, once again, better. The longboarder paddled in, saying he had to get back to Donegal, and others came and went, but it never got too crowded: feelings of cold, or stiffness, or anything else, all went away. Totally refreshed, totally stoked, totally transformed, we headed for a miniature feast at the local restaurant, complete with mulled wine by the fire, and watched some kind of rugby match on TV.

And still, even after such magic, the day wasn't over: a proposed move up the coast was foiled by a boggy patch of road: no worries at all, at all. Locals emerged, glad of the distraction: from a house across a field, children came to see if they could help. Tractors emerged, the golfers came out of their clubhouse: eventually mobile again, it was too late to head north, but instead an even more secret local wave awaited us: a peeling right, over a reef, hidden from view of the road.

Shooting the breeze with some windsurfers after the session, there was still time for one more stop: As Mossy refuelled, I had a look in to the festivities in the local pub, where some kind of birthday was in motion. Over a glass of Guinness, we were invited to stay, and were highly, highly, highly inclined to do so. Only the realities of the next day and the looming long drive home drew us away from the warmth and the music. Standing outside, we swapped confidences about the remote town with another visitor: don't tell anyone about it, we all agreed. If they are lucky enough, they might find it themselves – but, to be honest, they probably won't.

K-Bay on the Foamies

A little bit south of the usual lookout – up on the winding steps leading down to the beach, leaning on the green railing with the chipped paint – waves from the north were rolling in. I was seeing, just then, that it wasn't big, but it wasn't small either, and the way the break moved around with each different swell in those days kept you on your toes as well.

Reckoning there was a session in the making, we found a peak pretty far south, outside of the rocky point, and it was a wave for the foamies: big, and rolling, and needing all the volume and length and forgiveness in the world to get in amidst an ever-increasing crowd and the looming inside rocks as the tide dropped.

Mossy and I had a field day, laughing to ourselves at our good fortune. He reckoned the boards we had – super oversized lockdown-beater foamies – were getting us in at the very earliest point possible: the point at which the wave was maybe just even considering breaking. Sometimes, it felt as if the paddling and popping were even helping it to break, but maybe that was wishful thinking. We rode long and roping lefts and rights and peaks: it was another day of glory amidst the strangeness of the pandemic – another day when the waves made you forget it was there.

The GAA Pitch

On the road with Newstalk, the focus was on different spots, other places, once again: sure, there were waves at Easkey, but also crowds; it paid, he said – like he always said – to explore. I went with the flow, like I always did, because I now totally liked that vibe myself: liked the way that there were people who liked to sniff around and drive down side roads and dirt tracks to coastal recesses: liked all that, for sure, even if I felt a pang every time we drove away from the glories of Easkey right.

This time, we ended up at a left, known by various names, but most commonly the GAA Pitch or the Football Pitch: a bizarre name for a wave, it was a low tide spot that reeled down a shoal of shallow reef when it was on, racing and changing and doing all sorts of cool things. Today, the tide was dead low, exposing a shoal of deep brown bedrock reef: there, Newstalk met Ivan, an old surf hunter from previous missions, who seemed pretty happy to live in his van and chill and watch the waves.

Ivan, by himself, was quite a specimen: with a strong New Zealand or Aussie accent, he seemed to exist in that Miki Dora surfing netherworld of van-living-down-quiet-back-roads. There was, naturally, to the mainstream, always a question mark over such characters – but for some reason maybe slightly less in quasi-feral outreaches of the Wild West. Was he on the run from the law? Recently divorced? Broke? Or was he, maybe, all of the above? Or – or was he just a surfer, living the simple life, for as long as his body could take it?

I mean, it couldn't have been healthy, right? And yet the paradox was that you had, it seemed like, to be pretty healthy just to live like that: no baths or deep homestead comforts: the elements right outside your panel van sliding door; minimum security; a life lived pretty close to nature. Pretty close to the ruined stone building at the end of that lane that contained every kind of flotsam and jetsam you could imagine: pretty close to the ocean and the grass verge and the cows – and that, pretty much, was all there was.

For now, anyway, Ivan radiated health and confidence: sipped on his steaming mug of coffee, and may or may not have offered us one. With his sweatpants tucked in to his Ugg boots and his warm-looking fleece beneath a tanned and weathered face, he looked the part, and looked tough enough: as always, the antipodean accent lent something of the exotic to Sligo, though maybe not as much as it used to.

There, also we met Wayne, the founder of a short-lived Irish surf mag and former pro surfing judge; to complete the picture, a lady surfer from Donegal in a huge panel van showed up as well. And that was it, under the magical winter sun: deep, deep blue waves rose and reeled, and we all got our share, with no one else around. Ivan may or may not have faded me once or twice, but I am pretty sure it was by accident: he had clearly been living for the wave, and these kind of days, so I guess you had to factor that in as well.

Slabbage with Mossy

Eventually, Mossy and I ended up at the Slab: all other avenues had been closed, for sure, but even then it was a big gamble at the end of a surf trip. An extra hour's drive, and then an extra hour back home on top of it: it was driven, though – overpoweringly – by that end-of-trip feeling where you just don't really want to go home. So, no point in lingering: a surfer's logic will tell you the only thing to do, when perfecting the art of escapism, is to drive further away.

We ended up, then, at the end of a gravel road at the end of a headland at what still felt, twenty years later, like the end of the earth: the wide, open-ocean swells detonated against the tip of the point; fishing boats, colourfully painted, rocked and rolled across the ocean.

Out in the water, the sun shone, the tide was right. The swell was small but – because the wave was just as treacherous as it had been twenty years before – that didn't matter much. What was sort of important, though, was the fact that it was us, briefly, and then just one or two others: hooking waves in order, rotating, and everyone getting in a good groove. You had to: after standing up, a quick turn was required to avoid the reef, with sunlit brown seaweed sucking up the face and beneath your feet and before your eyes.

Somehow, no one hit the reef that day, and even the seaweed felt benign – felt like a potential cushion against the hard edges of the rocky slab. Each wave slanted and glinted in the setting sun, and stood up, and – more than anywhere else – broke along the contours of the land before imploding in the end section. And, for some reason, the green of the shore moss on the rocks – so treacherous to walk on – shone in the sun and glowed and radiated like a classic, unreal, vision of Ireland.

Back in the carpark, the veneer of chill faded fast: Mossy had pushed his time envelope, and even a brief moment of reflection in the parking lot was frowned on. We gun-lined it through the small towns, with the occasional squeal of brakes, before gun-lining it home – but the waves has given us the fuel we needed.

Kerry II

So much of Ireland, as I would later find with Hawaii – so much of the interactions, the read, the opportunity, the scene, the vibe – was shaped by the pandemic. But, after a particularly ugly lockdown, the shackles were off again as Newstalk and I headed back to Kerry: there was an ease, also, coming from the summer weather, and from an ancient-Irish sort of feeling of freedom and life and liberty, as we hit the road: the miles cruised by – this time no flat tires, no moments of existential angst – and we reached Inch in the early evening.

We weren't the only ones: scoping out a few options, we realised that everyone else had had the same idea, and were feeling the same thing. Most of the hostels felt overrun and overcrowded as a result: eventually, we ended up at the back end of Anascaul in a faux-thatch roof bed and breakfast run by some kind of cool Eastern Europeans.

We flipped on the room; Newstalk won, but gave me the one with the window that opened, which was cool of him. Soon after, we were in the South Pole Inn, eating lamb chops between plastic screens, and talking story, and trying to judge how the waves would be. Later, after he had crashed, I cruised back through the town, but there wasn't much on offer: the statue of Crean and his puppies beside the stream was about as much company as was going. Hey, probably for the best.

The next day, Newstalk lived up to his word and let me sleep: the tide wasn't going to work early in the morning. For once in a lifetime, then, even if only briefly, I felt rested on a surf trip: it wasn't to last, but it was nice to know that such a thing was even possible. From OMA to Mossy to Newstalk, all my fellow surfers always seemed to have some kind of preternatural ability to survive with little, or no, rest.

And so, leisurely, we drove past flat Annas, where he pointed out a hike across the fields and hills that led to a back bay wave, but which needed a big swell; at Inch, when we arrived, the surf was just – barely – delivering on the reef. But was also summer: no need for booties, or thick wetsuits, or all of the fear that winter engenders: there was no hesitation about taking a gamble, and seeing if there would be a push when the tide changed.

There wasn't – but a couple of runners still came through, and I caught a glimpse of what the real wave, in its prime, would actually look like: saw the shape and tapered end and feathering lips and the way it reeled down the cliffs. Learned some line up markers, chatted to some locals, soaked up the sun: checked the scenery, caught some waves.

After a while, stoked, I paddled the long way back in – to the beach and along the road and back to the car (I was, unlike Newstalk, no kind of mountaineer) and we sat and ate ice cream and checked out the local scenery in the sun. Maybe, possibly, Ireland whispered something that day: said not to go too far away, for too long, this time: said that there would be days like these, as good as anywhere in the world, on its shores.

Clare

To get this one point, like with most waves in Ireland, you have to drive. Then, after you have had a long drive, and then driven a little more – as the roads get narrower and windier, and as the rules of the road change to a more instinctive, country vibe – you have to park on an even narrower road; get changed in the ditch; wave to tourists and golfers in your cax; and then commando run, suitably dressed all in black, across a golf course. Then, when you have done all that, if it is on – and after you have gotten through the shorebreak that washes across a rocky ledge and keeps you right on your toes – you will be greeted by the usual splay of black dots, wetsuits bobbing up and down, fringing (and occasionally engulfed by) the action.

This was the sight that greeted Newstalk and myself: there was always the rush of adrenaline and fear, as well, heightened by the one other ledge of rocks that had to be clambered across and – seriously – by the fifty-foot-high plume of spray coming off the nearby cliffs, on even small swells, on the other side of the bay. And, as always, again – the icing on the cake – it was also first thing in the morning, and cold, post-cross-country mission: big, big sensory impacts for a sleepy traveller.

Coming back to Clare, like to anywhere in Ireland, had a mixed feel: these were the waves we invaded after wild nights in the old days: waves that usually defeated us, or that we got in to just by force of will, or hangovers, or *joie de vivre*, or just being twenty-five, or whatever. This time, there were no wild sessions in the local night club or hostel the night before, and I was maybe twenty years older – but the scene, otherwise, rock for rock and field for field, remained the same.

Some things were better, though: in surfing, animal cunning accumulates. Having been roughly schooled in many parts of world since last paddling out at an Irish point, I had learned a few tricks: at the start, sit a bit deeper – a bit more inside – and poach what you can get. Later, once you have broken your duck, and are loosened up, get in the mix with the outside crew – if they will let you.

And so it worked out: my first wave that day wasn't too far inside, and I felt ok to paddle for it after a little bit of repartee with some surprisingly friendly locals. (Had they got friendlier? Was it an age thing? Was I just maybe a better surfer? Was I just not hungover? Or had I, in the twenty years in between, just become as hardened as they had always been?)

Who knew: don't look a gift horse in the mouth; the important thing was that the steep and dizzying drop, where it seemed like the whole ocean lay before you, led in to a reeling wall, standing up as it broke evenly down the point. It was a moment of exhilaration – but also, seconds later, a feeling of the proverbial innermost limits of pure fun: the elevator feeling of seeing the surfer on the shoulder rise and disappear with the line of swell ahead of the field of vision; the good vibes and glimpses of smiles and moments of eye contact as you sped by.

After a lot of that kind of thing, and a lot of stoke, we met up back on land, and arranged to meet Mossy's brother, the Guru (who had turned out to be one of the black dots; that is Ireland for you) for lunch up the road. Feeling pretty good, and getting over the usual surf-plus-cross-country drive PTSD, I reckoned a glass of wine wouldn't go amiss, either. The Guru liked it; to be fair, I hadn't realised it was still morning. Then, back in the car: out of the roadside café, and hunting down the early afternoon session.

I probably could have taken it or left it, to be honest, but Newstalk wasn't buying that: he had had an indifferent session at the point, and wanted more. Going with the flow – as if I had a choice – we ended up at another bay – way southwards – where a few more black dots indicated there might be something on offer. There, he got his fill: in super-glassy, not-too-cold conditions, under overcast skies, a magical right reared up and peeled in the middle of the bay. What was it, though? Not a point, not a slab, not a beach – just some kind of middle-of-the-bay shoal, next to a sleepy village, and which was hugely influenced by the tide, and which broke once in a while.

My first waves, out there, felt magical: there was an island offshore, and a little sort of fly-fishing ripple on the surface of the water, and it all felt almost spiritual. The wave would wait just long enough to let you in before holding you in a pocket – allowing time, as well, for a turn before the end. All so, so good, but not for long: In Ireland, surf windows can be small. With every inch of the rapidly changing tide, the swell grew steeper, the water shallower, and the take-offs sketchier, until it was time to go in.

Meeting up back by the car, changing on another rainy roadside corner, it felt, immediately, like Newstalk had had his fill as well: I had seen him on a few, and he had gotten some nice ones, for sure. Eventually, we hit the long road home; one of the rare missions, I can tell you, where everyone went home happy.

Hawaii 3: The Fake Snake

Flying the flag on a Kimo Greene machine.

Re-Readjustments

Sometimes, for sure, getting away could be good. It could put Honolulu, and Waikiki, and Threes, into perspective: when you got back, it could make you feel like an alien landing from a spaceship, checking out the strange behaviour of earthlings.

It could help you cool off from Zach's critiques, as well: help you to sort of come at it fresh. After one trip, coming out of the ocean from a swim and seeing everyone at the showers, it felt like I was watching through a one-way mirror: felt like I had some kind of special capacity to open a portal into a different world. There they all were, doing their thing. Skipper Dave and Laurence, Zach and Chuck, showering and tarrying and shooting the breeze.

Hanging back and comparing rides and rinsing boards and trading notes; contemplating the session and considering the next one and just, generally – I reckoned as I strolled up to join them, and go through the looking glass again – just taking their time, shoots.

Spiritual Preparations

Is surfing really so spiritual? I don't know, based on what I have seen. In the right places, maybe – but there is also so much else going on: so much work, and activity, and repartee, and emotion, and wave-hunting, that to make it spiritual almost seemed to require a conscious effort.

Sitting out the back, in Hawaii or in Ireland, the tendency is not to reflect on the mysteries of the universe so much as hang tight and wonder what is for dinner, or what is swimming around you, or whatever else. So earthy, so material... So selfish, right? But, after some time trying to work it out, it seemed like the spiritual part was more to do with preparation than, as the military say, execution.

Thinking along the lines of football players who pick up a bit of grass, cross themselves, or look to the skies as they step across the white line, I tried to develop a few rituals of my own. A few moments of requests, or whatever else, in between waxing and changing and combing; in between putting on the leash, or changing the fins, or whatever. It seemed like there were enough challenges in Hawaii – the fish, the weather, the distance from shore, the crowds, the outbreaks of emotion – that I would be grateful for any kind of help I could get.

From there, other small rituals developed – moments of taking some of the shore water and touching it and saying a few words, or whatever. Moments, also, on bigger swells, of doing the same when leaving the water – of not leaving any assistance I received unacknowledged.

But there was a little more to it, as well. For sure, it was all just more selfishness, praying to get the best waves – but it was also about managing selfishness. Watching guys like Eddie and Chuck, it became clear that the best surfers had a different energy, and that there was such a thing as the most spiritual person in the lineup, even if I knew for sure that it was never going to be me. But, if I could take a step in that direction, it couldn't hurt.

In the end, it probably saved me. There were days out there when waves couldn't be had for love or money, unless one drifted your way – days when human will would only lead to frustration. "Let the waves come to you", or "pray for surf" would be the kind of cliché remarks that sort of fit the bill – but not quite. There was something else, as well – something Hawaiian. Something about the way the old school lads on big boards could sit out there, for an hour, maybe two hours, greeting people, showing some aloha, and only taking the occasional waves that came their way.

I hadn't really seen that kind of thing anywhere else, especially in the midst of such intensity. Maybe in Ireland – but there were other factors in play as well: in Hawaii, it was harder to contain the hunger for more and more of the aquamarine water, the warmth, the fluidity, the total joy of waves there.

So how did they do it, right? At a surfing memorial, I heard about how old school Waimea surfers like Peter Cole could sit and wait for hours at a time before choosing the right wave. Likewise, and maybe for the original Waikiki beach boys, there was that total lack of a sense of urgency as well – that lack of the squirrel collecting acorns sort of vibe; the lack of deadlines – the way it was the opposite; that you actually maybe wanted to slow things down a bit to extend your session. Whatever it was, less waves could sometimes mean more; short term sacrifices, as well, could earn you a better spot in the line-up in the end.

Living in Tourist Land

But what – or where – was the real Hawaii I was supposedly seeking, anyway? It didn't seem to be on my doorstep – or maybe it was; maybe, actually, that was exactly where it was. A place where things moved a little more slowly than on the mainland, as evidenced by the generally lazy pace of traffic along Saratoga: a military place, as illustrated by Fort DeRussy across the road. A place of locals, like Mike, whose pidgin repartee with whoever was passing would float through the apartment window as he was cleaning. And Hawaii, for sure, as a place of nature, with the roosters across the road squawking at all hours and having big families; with the plumeria tree outside my front door. But, above all, a place of tourists, brah.

Tourists: you have to love them. They live in such a bubble, and go through such madness, and badness, even while they are on holiday: even when they are where they want to be. In Hawaii, they don local outfits and get mocked and pay a lot and go on cruises and drink – and, generally, from what I could see, have the time of their lives. And they party and smoke and look around curiously and wander and wonder and bake, bake, bake in the sun: they eat out and stare at the ocean and get burned and get sandy and hog the showers, and then they go home.

They fight, and they have bad trips, and get stung by jellyfish, and cut themselves on the reef, and flail on surfboards, and look miserable some of the time. They float on big plastic rings in the ocean, they get tattoos. But, from most of what I saw, they were cool: for sure, things got totally out of hand the first year – that post-Covid summer, when the Pagoda went wild, and there were parties every night – those darkish days of domestic travel overload and release and revenge tourism, after people had been cooped up for a little bit too long – but better, more chill dynamics soon surfaced. Usually, the tourists brought a sense of peace and naïveté that was welcomed; that actually slowed things down even more.

I couldn't, honestly, say I didn't enjoy it. Touristland wasn't the idyllic visions of *Walking on Water*, but it wasn't the gloominess of *Welcome to Paradise* either: it was what it was, and that was a bubble, inside the broader Hawaiian bubble. It was nice, as well, after just a few months, to have people around me who knew even less than me: it was nice to adjust to the late-night noise of Waikiki, and to never really feel alone, no matter how much you occasionally wanted to. Nice to have that feeling of living in a holiday place; in a resort: nice to live that life – for a while.

But I can't, really, say it was the real Hawaii. No way. It was a side of it, for sure, but it maybe outweighed, too much, other parts: the realities of Ala Moana Beach Park and the East Side and the West Side; the communities and cultures of the windward and leeward. The inland empire cities, and the military bases; the darkness and the intensity of the North Shore; the old school benign menace of China Town and K-Town and Down Town – the other islands. The yuppie suburbs of Hawaii Kai and Kaimuki and Kaka'Apo and Kailua; the poor and semi-derelict high rises, with washing hanging from every balcony, over by the freeway.

Chuck's Sotto Voce

Chuck had cool ways of communicating, that was for sure. In lineups in which relations were ever changing – and which were sometimes liabilities – *sotto voces*, subtle signals, and even a glance in certain direction could speak volumes. It is the difference between acceptance and rejection; it is friendship or adversity. Chuck, being a king of the lineup, couldn't take any old straggler under his wing. I saw that, and I guess I would, for sure, have done the same thing in the Emerald Isle: in Hawaii, you had to be a hundred times more careful.

But, like I said, he had his ways. Even with adversaries out there – those who thought I had maybe moved in too fast, or too intensely, running under cover of pandemics and lockdowns – there were ways of getting hidden vibes across. At times when it would have been a bad choice for him to talk, he would just lift his chin, or point in a certain direction – or not, or just shake his head, or grimace, or something.

He was subtle, that is for sure: understated. And so, when he wanted to let the line up know that I was in the loop – part of the scene – he wouldn't greet me loudly: "Sebastian", he would say, "what time is it?" That was it: an acceptance; a message to the crowd. The surfers would, on some level, part as I called back that it was six-thirty, or whatever: the message had been broadcast; I was worthy of being asked what time it was – which was, in itself, a big thing.

He was no angel, and could even take some of my waves if he felt like it, and he would always tell you it had been good just before you got there. ("Paradise firing!" I said to him one day. "Was firing", he said. "'What is it doing now, then?" I asked. "Smoldering", he replied.) But – in some really vague, mercurial way – you just felt good with him in the water: secure, serene. And even on the beach, in a rush, you getting in and he getting out – there was time for some guidance. "Sit wide", "Sit inside" – some kind of signal. A shake of the head, to give you the inside track even before you paddle out: A *sotto voce*: a mumbled phrase that would put you, maybe, briefly, in pole position.

Cunningham Soirée

Even at the party, he was still a lifeguard: up at Cunningham's for a charity sort of thing, Zach and I admired the views from his partner's place and reflected on a guy who had done a lot of good things for people; reflected on the way that indirectly, maybe, these sort of moments were part of his own karma: rewards for a pretty hard life in the sun, doing good things for – let's face it – mainly dumb strangers whom he didn't know and who, often, Darwin might have had other plans for. It had been a winding road for him to get to that point, from what I could gather, but he looked comfortable and at ease amidst the opulence – as if, somehow, he could see beyond it: as if he knew this was all part of the big picture.

The funny part, though, was that Cunningham was, at heart, even in such elegant settings, still a lifeguard: not for him the sitting back and drinking wine kind of vibe; not for him the pupus and repartee – well, maybe a bit. But, at heart, the cool thing was that, essentially, he was still on duty, as he was hard-wired to be: still checking out the scene, and looking for sign of distress, and basically making sure that everyone was safe, and relaxed, and having a good time.

The other thing about Cunningham, I was starting to think, was that he kept himself – not just through surf, or art, so much – but, somehow, kept himself relevant. Not through his superstar bodysurfing legacy, so much as via some other, slightly more ethereal thing. It was, maybe, the way he was able to bridge the cosmic vibe of surfing – which dealt with the interconnectedness of all things, and karma, and jungle juice, and all that kind of thing – with real people, and the real world. With, if I can use the world, the blue-collar world, of which lifeguards were for sure a part.

Because, let's face it, surfers live in a bubble, and a lot of people might, if they ever had to listen to a surfer for too long while they are thinking about paying the rent, or their nightmare commute, or their shift at the factory, or whatever, sort of start to dislike the surfer who was speaking. But Cunningham, somehow, bridged that gap. Transcended it, and made the hippy dippy part accessible and attractive and real, even to the man in the street: Cunningham, somehow, managed to bridge the transcendence of the surfer with the vox populi: he would never make the spiritual mistake of looking at life, and the world, and people, through the eyes of the entitled.

The Forecasts and the Crowds

Who would be a surf forecaster? It has to be, possibly, probably, one of the worst jobs in the world. Sure, they make money, from what I hear – and, because of their virtual nature, they are pretty much untouchable. Veiled by a level of anonymity, surfers are also, generally, too relaxed to follow up on bad forecasts; they are, surfers and forecasters alike, more often than not just on to the next swell, with not too much time for the rear-view mirror (unless you want to tell someone you missed it).

In Hawaii – like with everything to do with surfing – things got exaggerated, magnified, and blown out of proportion. The forecasters would predict a flat spell and there would be waves: they would call for a big swell, and hype it up, and call it a day to target – big time, totally unmissable – and the waves would trickle through. And the forecasters, more than anyone, were responsible for that big, big thing at Threes: The surfer-to-wave ratio.

It was the days when that was off, when it was maybe three or four surfers to each wave, that things got a little gnarly. Impatience, dirty moves, boredom, frustration, the dark arts: each would surface in the simmering line up. It was bad, for sure – though maybe not as bad as it once had been: older hands told me that, in the years before the hotelisation, the privatisation, of Waikiki – and the parking issues, and all the rest – the crowd used to, bizarrely, be way worse. In the old days, the stevedores were the enforcers, Tom told me one evening: they would happily break the fins off your board and send you in if you transgressed. Today, there was less order, less structure, more forecasts, more cameras: nice, but also terrible; a true double-edged sword.

Anyway, the forecasters: When they said it was a day to target, my heart sank. All you could do would be to hope it wasn't going to be a day of one-wave sets, or long lulls, or whatever: not to sound misanthropic, but clouds and wind and rain would, happily, help to keep people away, as well. But, usually, the crowd would take the forecasters at their word: the crowd would pretty much ignore the option, a lot of the time, of just looking at what was actually out there.

There was an exception, though, and he was so, so cool. A sort of hole in the wall internet forecaster on an obscure website, Pat Caldwell got overlooked by a lot of the mainstream forecasting acolytes. Zach had told me about him, and I signed up, and he told it like it was. No doubt, there was an element of the mad professor in there as well: You could, for sure, see him poring over charts and historical databases and New Zealand weather forecasts, and pretty much the kitchen sink as well. But he wanted to help, not to hype: to make sure the right people got in the right lineups on the right days.

The best part, though, was Wooly the Worm: Caldwell's mystical forecasting creature, whose dreamy antics would help to let the massif know what was on the horizon. Some days, he would be at Pau Hana at Rat Worm's Sports Bar: if he had one too many and danced on the counter and fell off, well, that would be a bad sign for the surf (after maybe a flurry of storm swell). If he was doing yoga with his friend, Clarissa Catapilla – maybe on top of a compost heap – and touched his toes one too many times and fell over, that might mean a pulse that stretched out a bit. It was, to say the least, a nice way of putting it.

Pistol Pete and the Fake Snake

Who knows what to say about Pete? That he never had a last name? That he was half-real? Probably the same as what he would say about me – which is something I don't know, but sort of think, would be the same: someone little resistant to categorisation, maybe, but, at the same time, sort of a cliché – in a good way.

Pete had long hair, and he was from Florida, and he was pretty far out in that stoned surfer sort of way, and chatted it up in abstract and *non sequitur* sorts of ways in the lineup. Most importantly, though, was that he wanted to go left – the lesser option, most of the time – even though he was a shortboarder; even though he was always in the right spot; and even though he could surf quite a bit.

So, that was cool: With the guys and gals who went left, all you had to do, sometimes, was sit deep and line yourself up with them. With Pete, though, it hit another level – we would exchange winks and nods and subtle calls and signals, and it became a pretty funny, pretty cool, thing. Up to a point, of course: abusing the system would, for sure, make it all fall apart.

But we loved it – or at least I did. It wasn't a snake, which would be bad, the way he and I paddled around. Instead, it was a fake snake; a move where it looked like you were totally burning or offending the very person you were actually working with. A bluff and a double bluff: a three-card trick where you both won; a dodge, and a crowd beater, and a trick of the trade.

Banalities

Like with anything, anywhere, Hawaii wasn't all about the sublime and the transcendent and the radical and the different. There were practicalities, banalities: there was food shopping, there was laundry. There was working out how not to pay triple the price for things when you were in tourist land; there was figuring out how to summon the energy to wash your clothes in the midst of the heat and the lethargy.

The food shopping, after a while, was pretty much ok. I found a place called Food Pantry at the other end of town, where real people shopped, but where you didn't need to undertake some sort of mind-bending super shop or mall mission; over time, also, diet improved and became more Hawaiian, I guess you could say. More avocadoes, and more rice: more noodles, but, also for sure, a shift to less processed food and less additives, all that kind of thing – anything to give you some kind of clean feeling amidst the heat and the sun and the sleepiness and the languor that the tropics could bring.

Laundry, in its own way, was cool. Well, maybe not cool: when you got the hang of it, it was easy though. If no one stole your clothes from the washing machine, which had been known to happen, there was no need for dryers; instead, everything out on the balcony air dried within maybe an hour or two. If there was one small thing about Hawaii that trumped every other small thing, it was that: the way you could dry clothes in a few hours was just something that, for whatever reason, made me feel very stoked, very consistently.

Maybe, also, the ease had something to do with Hawaiian dressage: let's face it, you don't need much in the way of clothes in Hawaii. You need shorts and t-shirts and flip flops and something respectable to wear to work, for sure: you needed to keep things clean, and presentable, and all that kind of thing – but you sure didn't need much. No coats, gloves, hoods, sweaters: no hats, scarves, or, yeah, underwear. If you wore it, you would suffer: no amount of aspirations to style, apart from maybe the occasional pair of jeans, could justify the pain involved with the additional layers.

Rewind III: Covid Ireland

Covid desolation.

Covid Checks

Standing looking over the ocean – some time in, say, early 2020 – somehow the lockdown didn't matter so much anymore: the surf check had become part of the daily routine; a part of mid-morning life – and bizarrely, magically, there has been a lot of surf. Cross-checking tide with swell and wind, and just generally soaking up whatever sun there was, the image of right-handers rolling in again from the north was a compelling one: a man asked me why I wasn't already out there; I told him I was waiting for the tide. Just go, he said – and he was right.

So began weeks of local waves: the population of K-Bay swelled dramatically. It was this sort of secret thing; this sort of suspicious thing; but also this sort of Covid-untouchable thing. There was only one fear, that overrode the joy: that beach access would be cut off, and we would lose our lifeline. At times, it almost felt that was what some people, who were maybe having a little bit of a harder time than we were, wanted – who were we to be frolicking when the world was imploding around our ears, Apocalypse Now style?

But the days went by, and the beaches stayed open – and we kept surfing, and checking the waves, and patched together some good, good times amidst the fear and the chaos and the media frenzy. On the mid-morning surf checks, familiar faces would appear, and we would shoot the breeze while trying not to touch supposedly infected railings. Those checks were moments of lingering languor – of feeling like you might just want for another five minutes to see if a set came through, just to be sure.

Country Road

For whatever reason, Newstalk and I ended up on a back, back, back road somewhere on the Sligo-Mayo border. Just another nameless country road, I guess – though maybe it had a local title, or a number on a map – on the way to a surf check. But there was a very, very cool part to it, as well: it was the kind of place that you would never, ever be in, for any reason, unless you were going to check the surf. That, for sure, will always be one of the most magical parts of surfing in Eire – being where you would never otherwise be; where no one could find you: where you were, briefly, off the grid.

Anyway, on that road, we saw Foamie parked, and pulled up beside him. He had been on a similar hunt, and had seen different things, so there was information to be exchanged. Like two group of Arabs meeting in the desert – and as a local dog sniffed around us and cows stood staring in the background – we compared notes, and strategised, and shot the breeze.

Amidst the green fields and stone walls, however, there was no real burning desire to move fast, either. The dog sniffed some more, and we chatted some more, and topics drifted around – what were our plans; where were we headed in life; what had we had for breakfast? What was that unusually-shaped surfboard in the back of Foamie's car – one that he had shaped himself, it turned out, leading on to a whole new conversation.

And so it went on, until some invisible internal timer chimed – driven, maybe, by a distant plan or promised return hour; or the need to beat the tide; or the sun coming out; or the sun going in; or maybe rain; or whatever. But for those few minutes – for that half an hour – it was a moment in the alternate universe of Irish surf trip time: off the radar; possibly even out of cell phone coverage; a covert coterie. No one, nobody, rushing or hassling or demanding deadlines or products – out there, the opposite was true. For sure, you had to have something to show for your efforts, surf wise – but it would have been a big mistake not to stop and smell the flowers along the way.

Big, Windy Lefts

At Easkey, the wind howled as the lefts broke and a continental shortboarder managed the tumult with finesse. The sun shone but I couldn't get into the groove; it was too windy and wild and loose; I had been pampered by SF for too long.

Lockdown with Mossy the Guru

Sometimes, for sure, nothing worked out. Even with every possibility covered – every map and forecast explored – there remained the possibility the swell wouldn't come through: that the wind would be wrong, or the interval wasn't right, or the weather wouldn't work, or – worst of all – that we were, deep down, deceiving ourselves. That we had convinced ourselves that the mission would be worthwhile: that the odds were in our favour, even though they weren't.

So when the Guru and Mossy and I wound up on a cottage near a certain wave, and the rain beat down in the dark, and we sat back and maybe opened a bottle of whiskey or two, there was always the risk that the next morning wasn't going to work out. We tried, for sure, to believe that it would, and make plans accordingly: but we also knew, for sure, that it was likely to be an all-or-nothing occasion.

The call, when it came the next morning, was a tense one. The Guru, careless of cold and hangovers and rain, had made a pre-dawn reccy to check the point. Mossy, lying on a couch and looking pretty relaxed, tensed up: we waited, and Mossy said, "oh no", and I knew – just knew – that it wasn't on. Not only that, but that it wouldn't be on tomorrow or the next day, either: that the storm had settled in, and the rain was here to stay, and we were, for sure, going to move to plan B, or C, or D, or whatever nuclear option we could come up with.

It was barely worth it, but Mossy and I headed to double check that the Guru wasn't just bluffing: that he wasn't maybe attempting some kind of bizarre feint to score a few waves no his own. He wasn't: though the curve of the bay was there, the swell dribbled in across the rocks and faded on the shore.

There was, though, still the other spot: a reef that picked up a smaller swell nearby. A wave that was, right then, pretty much in the eye of the storm: the bay was riven by wind and spray and rain and everything else, pretty much, that the elements could throw at us.

That, for sure was no deterrence: using group foolhardiness dynamics to do things that we would never have done on our own, we took the plunge and surfed. On bigger boards, we tried not to get blown back off the lines of swell as we were paddling in: a new kind of performance metric was developed, right then, that had more to do with how well you could hold any kind of line in the storm than with anything else.

The question, though, wasn't how you could try to make it tolerable: it was, bizarrely, why it was even enjoyable. Why were we having a good time – how could anyone feel stoked on the middle of the Irish winter, in the middle of a storm? There was an answer, I reckoned: who cared why you were enjoying it, you just were. Maybe it was the hardship, or the mates, or the sheer bizarre nature of it all: but the mere fact that you were stoked to be there, for whatever reason, said it all: if you were – and we were – then Ireland is for you, mate. Because if you can enjoy that, you are pretty much good to go for most of the other parts, if you play your cards right.

I paddled in early, running back to try and beat the lads to the shower for the hottest water. On the way back, the Guru swept past me in his car: we laughed, later, about the temptations to take others out, just for a bit of heat, when push came to shove.

Glassy Outside Left (to the Left of the Left)

On an overcast but not-too-cold in-between sort of day, somewhere in spring or autumn, the three of us sat at an odd spot, around a corner from a river mouth (and a more established wave). The waves were ultra-glassy – and only us, maybe one or two others, and a British guy and his son were out. Mossy and Newstalk and I sat under the grey clouds and talked and surfed.

It wasn't a day of significance or consequence: just lovely, beautiful, unique, sublime, green-grey-black Irish waves with your mates. Nothing really happened. I got a few, they got a few – I think Mossy maybe had a bad day, but not too bad. The waves came our way, and we had time to laugh in between sets. And, that pretty much, was about it: a session that would likely go unremembered were it not for conditions and company.

The Worst Journey in the World

Nothing, pretty much, was worse than that. It wasn't physical, and it wasn't about Covid, or about travel – it was, more like, some kind of perfect storm space in between worlds: waiting in an airport to start something new, and possibly bad; ending a year in Ireland where I felt pretty stoked most of the time; and ending, for sure and for ever, San Francisco. It was also my first time on a Covid plane, right at that point: right at the end of an era and the start of a new one, multiple worlds colliding – sudden ends of regimes and routines, and change in climates, and a return to all the old, old gnarliness of travels that had accumulated over the years. It was, pretty much, a rough moment – even for a surfer, heading to Hawaii.

Last person through the door, and last person on board – but a whole row to myself because, let's face it, the world was still pretty much a ghost town at that moment in time. And – now I come to think of it – to be fair, it maybe wasn't the worst journey: It couldn't have been, because I had that whole row to myself, and the plane was half empty, so I seriously can't complain.

Normally, in that sort of situation, I would do certain things: Drink wine, and watch movies, and read books – just sort of enjoy it. Chill out and change in to shorts and sleep and roam the aisles and stretch; talk to the cabin crew, if they were friendly, and just engage in that whole painless and quasi-enjoyable travel routine. But I had put down roots in Ireland, and was heading in to the unknown: I had nothing in place for my arrival – not even a place to stay in Honolulu – and basically just wasn't in the mood for any of it. But a year at home had maybe been enough, and if I didn't check out Hawaii now, the chance wasn't going to come back again.

But it wasn't easy: the change, and the end of the hibernation, and the circumstances, and all the rest of it, added up. I lay there, with my face mask hurting my ears, and stared at the seat – and that was pretty much it. For ten hours, pretty much everything shut down – apart from my actual consciousness, apart from questions: would I get waves, meet people? What about sharks, and locals, and getting the right board; what about the sun and the work and the remoteness of it all? I wasn't even thinking about my surfboards; wasn't even travelling with them. It was that bad – but at least I was, somehow, on the way to Hawaii.

Hawaii 4: War Paint

Peace amidst the battle.

Makapu'u with Cunningham

There was something preternaturally cool about cruising, in Hawaii, with Cunningham – that is for sure. Nothing overt: noting that you could really put your finger on – just a general sort of vibe that suggested ease, efficiency, and many other benign things. I guess if you are heading out to the windward side early on a Saturday with a pretty famous lifeguard from one of the most lethal surf breaks in the world, you end up feeling like you are in safe hands.

But it wasn't just a bodysurfing expedition: en route, stopping to check Sandy's, I learned about what it was like to grow up in Hawaii; twists and turns, personal and professional; learned nicknames (Captain Dilly Dally) and a tendency for absurdist humour; learned how lucky lifeguards are with parking; and listened to a few tales from the shorebreak as well. I asked him where he wanted to go in the world: he said he didn't really have a burning desire to go anywhere, actually. That, I have to say, was the first time I had heard that one from anyone, anywhere. What was with this Hawaii place, anyway?

We drove on to Makapu'u; parked at the overlook; scrambled down a cliffside sand path. Before the bodysurfing – or maybe it was after – there came a sort of early morning ritual rubbish pick up: he was not only doing it for a beach that he loved, but for raw materials for eco-sculptures, as well. We ended up with a lot: stashed it, and then hooked a few waves.

What can I say – I was careful not to crowd the guy. I mean, in surfing terms, he was famous. He knew I wrote books, and you sometimes feel that you don't want to abuse that by asking too many questions – even though I wanted to. I wanted to ask about the trauma and the stress, and if his eyes hurt from staring at the ocean for most of his waking life: about risking his life to save people who had ignored safety advice; about the thresholds, when you say to the punter: "Hey, buddy, you are on your own if you go out there". I for sure wanted to know if dealing with dead swimmers or surfers had affected him – but the conversation never went down that road, and I sort of felt that he didn't necessarily want it to.

The morning wasn't over – as an honoured invitee to his brunch, I met his wife, and talked about Covid and epidemics and lockdowns After, he dropped me back to Waikiki: the day felt oddly perfect, sort of self-contained – as if I had been on a tour, or something. But it wasn't like that: Mark was being kind and hospitable, free of charge: just being a lifeguard, and looking out for people on land as much as he would on water. Sometimes there is no agenda; no quest, no nothing: just, as he said himself, "show up and be kind".

Black Board Shorts at Night

Despite the benign minimalism of Hawaiian life, you could work the style angles as well: you surely could. You could have aloha shirts that were maybe a little less garish, a little better fitting; you could avoid the matching shorts and shirt – that was for sure – which looked like grown-up infant pyjamas. You could, maybe, have different boardshorts for different occasions: you could, if you wanted, have black board shorts and white shirts at night, if you felt like it.

You could have a cleaner pair of flip flops for outings, and you could be a little bit more careful of how your toenails looked, if you wanted to look sharp: you could keep a pair of good jeans in store, and a clean white pair of tennis shoes, if things got really formal. You could sport a flower or a lei or a bracelet – you could fix your hair, and scrub up, and hit the bright lights of Honolulu on a post-surf high. Or, for sure, you could also just throw whatever you found on and, salt and sand-encrusted, and make your way to a post-surf pint on a flood of adrenaline and stoke.

The Californians

For whatever reason, amongst the tourists, the Californians couldn't really hang. The rest of the mainlanders, for sure, could hack it – but the Californians, well, they were a different story, brah. They came in droves, and loved the vibe, and the sun and the warm water: they had money from the tech valley and fancied themselves, totally rightly, as super progressive.

But Hawaii, underneath it all, wasn't always that politically correct. And so they could get wrong footed too easily – and where were the freeways? Where were, like, the options of going to biker bars, or Burning Man, if they felt that particular impulse? Where was Yosemite – where was Lake Tahoe? And why, they would ask – even though they are super laid-back Californians – why didn't people actually turn up even remotely on time? What was Hawaiian time? Why was all this tropical paradise straining the Californian relaxation gene – why was this making them feel a little bit uneasy; why were they waiting, and waiting, and no one would call to say where they were?

Yes, shoots, it was funny: the Californians got wrong footed, very easily, in Hawaii. They weren't, to be honest, as relaxed, maybe, as they thought they were – or as they used to be: these days, with all their wealth and health, they weren't as patient or as dreamy or in touch with nature, maybe. They had, like, important things to do in the world of tech: they felt, maybe, a little cut off in a place that ostensibly had nothing, really, beyond what they had themselves back in the Golden State – maybe a little less.

Don't get me wrong: I love Californians, and nearly became one: they stand for a lot of good things, and set good tones, and like music and tolerance and cooperation. They showed up well in Ireland, and in Africa, whenever I meet them there – and they numbered amongst good mates, and good surfers – like Igor, and Christian, and Liam – they were, almost always, good people. It was just Hawaii that seemed to confuse them: just that Hawaii, for some reason, caught them off-guard, and made them sweat, and made them pine for the mainland.

Pulling In

The deeper waves, when they came my way on the third day of the May swell – the first real swell of the second year – were hard to find amidst the crowd: dropping in, setting up – after the usual Formula One-esque bun fight for position and priority – I could see, out of both peripheral and direct vision, nothing but bodies. There were, thus, on a big and steep wave, only two real options – or maybe, max, three: surf over them, make them pay; straighten out and pass on the wave and live in regret and resentment – but be a good person; or pull up into the wave, hit the gas, and go, go, go.

The way my new board from Kimo was riding – the way it was easier to move around the wave, and had a rounder tail, and a more fluid outline – it was the third option that prevailed: as the wave walled and curled ahead of me, I glimpsed multi-coloured spots of humanity scratching for the shoulder, or ditching boards, or duck diving, or just sitting there looking on. There was really no other choice, but it put your heart in your mouth (as they say in Ireland): everything felt so fractional, so balanced, and right on the very fine line between control and loss of it: controlling everything one could, controlling the controllables, but, at the heart of it all, also pretty much giving in to the ocean, and the wave, and the situation, and hoping that it would work out.

Bring your Guns to Town

"He was right here", said Chuck, pointing at a patch of water two yards or so away. "right there". Sitting out the back, Chuck was telling me how it went down. The way he told it, and I am sure that is what happened, is that Big Orange and he were paddling out, out, out. Orange thought he saw a boat wake coming, and Chuck too; gradually, maybe Chuck first, they realised that the wake had amplified the big set even further. "That is not a wake", Chuck said to Big Orange.

Then, as it always does, a lot of things happened at once: both registered what was happening; both looked at each other;

questions about who was going (Orange, despite being from out of town, had priority, and Chuck was way too cool a guy to fade him); choices were made. In front of his eyes, Chuck saw the wave being taken, and ridden, but not ridden perfectly: he got caught too deep, and didn't make it all the way.

What can you say? That it was a complement to the wave, as it always is, that the big boards turned up – that out of town-ers turned up? That North Shore people paid attention? Maybe – but also, maybe, it was also exactly that sort of technicolour day at the circus: an 11′8″ orange gun turned up on a day when the blues were so blue, the sky so radiant, the sea so alive.

War Paint

Anything for an edge: sooner or later, though, it gets a little extreme. But I had watched Chuck for months with his sunglasses on, protecting his eyes from the radically harsh ocean tropical glare: why not, I reckoned one day, and ever-mindful of the health-obsessed Hawaii surf culture – why not try it out? Protect your vision! Stop yellow eyeballs! And all the rest…

Not via sunglasses, though – too techy, too likely to lose them – so something else: what about the eye black used by sportsmen – baseball and American football players and goalkeepers – to stop light reflecting up off the surface, on to the cheekbone, and into the eyes? What about some black stripes across the cheeks, maybe?

A little research showed that it had only minor effects in terms of eye protection, but there were other agendas bouncing around in my mind. In Hawaii, home of the tattoo, a little eye black goes a long way; for a split second, you are the extreme one who maybe, just maybe, got a tattoo on your face. On closer inspection, when the mere makeup is revealed, the effect remains: there is a hint, just a hint – in that most ancestral of cultures – of war paint.

Almost always, though, people just laughed. 'Got your game face on!" some surfers said to me, more than once, as they paddled past. It also had a habit, towards the end of a session, of streaking down my cheeks, further lessening the desired warrior effect. But – on a big swell – in some way, it seemed to fit. It was a mark of respect to the waves; a salute to the occasion; and a sign that you were out there for the long session. Mitch, on the beach, used to judge the waves, and the day, based on the number of stripes I would put on: "Sebastian! A three-stripe day! Nice!"

As Good as Any

What were the biggest, swells, the best swells? One thing was for sure – you hadn't been there for them, and had never seen their like, and never would – even if you had been out there pretty much every night for a couple of years, and had for sure been there for big swells that passed through.

What I mean is that there was always, rightly, the mythical: the out-of-control days you only ever heard about, like when Three's broke over by Four's, or Kamehameha day 2013, or another landmark once-in-a-decade event. It was a fair call, and a right one: if ever you wanted your mind blown, and to see a place maxing out or at its wildest or biggest or baddest or most beautiful, chances are you would have to spend your whole life there. And, no doubt, some people did.

There were exception to that vibe as well, though. One day when checking the surf, Ralph and I discussed the last big swell that had come through. "That" he said while gazing at the ocean, "was as big as anything. As good as anything, as serious as anything".

I liked the idea, even though there were probably too many gradations; even though he was probably just being nice. Even though there was a good chance that the best sets ever at Three's might have come through in the middle of the night; even though Chuck only gave that swell a seven; even though tide or direction or wind or sun or colours or period or shape or angle – might have been just marginally off. The truth was, no one person would ever be there for the best day, right? All you could do would be to sniff around the edges; the shadowlands; the simile of the cave; and hope you got a sense of what really could happen.

The Dark Arts

For sure, it wasn't all peace and love and patience. Over time, yeah, the waves would come your way – but not always, and not always when you wanted them. Over time you would get things dialled in, or be given waves, or develop a sixth sense, or be on good terms with enough people to tune in to some exceptions to the rule book. But sometimes you had to see it as gladiatorial and Darwinist: sometimes, on the busy days, you had to use every trick in the book.

I was never the type, or in the position, to get aggro, but there were work-arounds: Kimo's boards were the biggest cheats of all, getting me in earlier and deeper than many of those who dropped in on me unintentionally could ever expect. But there were other subtleties, as well: not getting too deep into conversation, not taking your eyes off the horizon.

And watch the current, and have your line up markers dialled: who would have thought, Pavlov style, that the angle side wall of the distant Waikiki Shores building would have such profound meaning for me (or the way the end of Diamond Head hit that particular part of a particular building, or the way the edge of the Sky Bar lined up with the end of the Sheraton at Paradise). These weren't really dark arts, I guess – but I sure wasn't sharing my education.

And, let's be honest: there were flag of convenience repartee; there was back paddling. There was paddling out to the top left corner, and then diagonally back to the right inside corner: there were paddle battles, and eye contact, and no eye contact, and competitive strategies. There was dismissiveness of newcomers, and tight lips, and retreats, and constant scanning of the inside to see who was there that mattered: there were hierarchies to respect, and hierarchies that had to be challenged, and invisible lines of communication. There was one set of rules for some, and another for others.

But the reality was that, if you were cool and respectful and humble and patient, as well as being just plain human, you would be ok. Stop and say hi to people as you paddle out; encourage those who were struggling. Give waves away; eat humble pie; stay out after dark. Pray and wait and try to stay spiritual: be prepared for days when you were going to be short changed. Try to bring good vibes into the lineup, watch and learn, and pick your battles: don't get greedy, and work on your karma – and, most of the time, and you would get what you wanted – or, at the very least, what you deserved.

The Funeral and the Jam

But the real Hawaii? The real, real Hawaii? Well, I guess you should go to a funeral, or something: that is pretty real, right? It sure seemed that way as I got out, with Mike, at his brother Vince's funeral, at the Valley of the Temples, on an Oahu mountainside. Felt that way, for sure, as I saw the different styles of dress: anything from biker jackets to alohas shirts to mohawks – and, for sure, felt that way as I queued up to drop off a card and pay respects to family before entering the chapel.

There, you learned more: heard the stories from relatives about growing up in Hawaii and how people needed protectors, or 'amakuas, or however you wanted to describe it: how the bigger lads helped out their brothers, and how families had uncles everywhere, and how families lived together in two-up, two down arrangements, and how brothers and cousins were pretty much the same thing.

And the music, and the dancing, and the tears – but also the positivity, and the optimism: Hawaiian funerals were light, floral affairs, and reflected spirituality, for sure, and could not have been more different from their Irish counterparts: no gloominess and greyness and darkness; a minimum of formality and a maximum of colour. I had to get back to work, so disappeared before things escalated: Mike told me the next day that the guitars came out and the day turned into night as they sang and played and drank and saw his brother off, local style.

The Peter Cole Memorial

It was North Shore Hollywood: at Peter Cole's memorial – a big wave North Shore environmentalist – I actually sort of found it too much. It was early in the morning and I wasn't, in any way, at my best: amidst the crowds, I cruised down to the Sunset Beach shoreline and swam and reflected on the walk from Pipeline to the tents with Cunningham, who had kindly picked me up and brought me there earlier that morning.

Between the two parking lots, he regaled me, casually, with the stories of pretty much every house: who lived where and what Jack Johnson was doing with his yard, and where the big parties were, and all of that. There was Fred Pattachia in his driveway; you could see he loved Mark and we shook hands and, briefly, shot the breeze.

Yes, for sure, it had been a lot to take in: and so away from the too cool for school, sunglasses-in-the-shade funeral element – but, even on the beach, Ken Bradshaw paddled up, arriving by surfboard, and asked me if the thing had started yet – he had been delayed, he said, waiting for a refrigerator delivery. Would I have wanted, I wondered, looking into his eyes, to have been Bradshaw's refrigerator delivery man? I wasn't sure; it seemed like a lot of pressure, particularly if anything went wrong.

Back at the ceremony, Cunningham saved me seat at the front: I sat, on the other side, between a super hippy North Shore Mama and a lot of her youngsters who just chilled out and stared at me occasionally. Clyde Aikau made a speech: Buzzy Kerbox, for some reason, was staring right at me. No, wait, he was staring at Mark: who cares, this was, for sure, the real thing. On the way home, super stoked, we ran into Jock Sutherland who stopped his car and leaned out of the window and said he loved Ireland and Irish whiskey and that he was a roofer. I told him not to combine the whiskey and the roofing too much, and he laughed, and we walked on.

Health is Wealth

I was finding, as well, that there were other ways to survive in Hawaii – other necessities, that wouldn't have been required or pursued elsewhere. For one thing, the constant demands of the surfing life – pretty much every day in the water, for an hour, or maybe two, or maybe more – required a little extra effort when it came to keeping body and soul together.

As a result, my bathroom shelf began to resemble a laboratory: turmeric, bromelain. Zinc, cranberry, Niacin, cod liver oil: fibre, and vitamins for the eyes and the ears and the teeth. Tubes of arnica and Topricin to ease sore muscles: sinus rinses, and eye washes, and a host of other natural remedies.

Surfing took other efforts, as well: I had been told by physical therapists that I needed to be more careful when it came to exercises, and so developed a small armoury of Therabands, leg weights, foam rollers. Routines would vary according to the ailment in question – but, either way, every couple of days, at least half an hour would be devoted to strengthening and stretching and rolling out elusive and problematic surfing muscles and joints.

Pops needed arms; surfing needed healthy legs and a core. Surfing, also would tilt you out of alignment, and the constant straddling of the board in between sets took its toll on the hips. Your neck, arms, knees all needed to be in trim: it was a life constantly on the edge of one injury or another, constantly trying to pull back before a twinge turned into something else and – worst thing of all, bra – put you out of the water for a while.

Zach's Gone – Zach's Back

Gradually, things settled. There was, honestly, a period of maybe a month where we just didn't even talk to each other – apart, maybe, from the occasional lineup grunt. For sure, I had been greedy; for sure, Zach was pretty far out sometimes. Maybe it was also just one of those island phases: you get sick of someone, ignore them, then realise you are both on the same island and sort of just get on with it. Same as in Ireland: I knew the vibe.

It saved time, that was for sure: I would avoid the showers, and head home solo, and not hang back for a catch up or a stroll or talking story, or anything. At that moment in time, it suited both of us: Zach wanted to get back into the groove of hanging with Chuck and the lads, and stop being a charity for floating surfers; I wanted more scope to do my own thing and – maybe as a result of that – it was a pretty basic stage in the evolution of the scene. Still, it was a pity that it had gone that way, for sure: I knew surfers, and how temperamental they could be, and it felt like a bit of an impasse that wasn't likely to be fixed any time soon.

And so it was cool when the text arrived: a few lines about maybe we should try to get on a bit better, even though I never listened to anything anyone told me; even though he was trying to help. That was true: but, at the same time, you need filters: not everything everyone said was right, not even with Zach – and, kids, it is always that way. But, looking back, I can say for sure that some of the nuances of his perorations – some of the details about hanging back and playing the long game and not taking every wave that came my way – were right, and were part of Hawaii, and were not things that I had even believed in, or tuned in to, before.

So, at the end of the day, Zach meant well, and I think he really, deep down, wanted things to work out for me, but – like with anyone – you had to take some things with a pinch of salt. Like with anyone, what they thought was good for you didn't always align with what was actually good for you, in the big picture: like with anyone, he was right pretty much about half, about fifty percent, of the time when he was giving advice. The problem was that he gave so much advice to so many people that the odds of him being wrong – just like the odds of him being right – were, maybe, a little higher than others.

He could get incensed: once, at the showers, he made the unusual move of throwing his leash at me. There were periods when there was no chat, no walk back home along Saratoga talking about

Italian politics, or whatever: but those moments passed, and he cared, and he was passionate about what he cared about: and that was, despite the inaccuracies and the tirades and the political discourses, pretty much enough.

Forgetting the Keys (Every Day)

No question, as well, that Hawaiian waves could spin you out. Not always in bad ways: the warmth of the water, the colours of the evening sunset, the ripples and curls and noise and emotion and all-encompassing vibes of the lineup – they would stay with you, taking over other parts of your brain, dominating your synapses, and generally leaving you with that sort of dumb, cliché-surfer expression of blankness mixed with the cosmic.

It was, almost always, a cool feeling – though it had its drawbacks. At one stage, I started stashing my keys on the beach – while watching out for big tides and metal detectors, and all that kind of thing. The idea was just to avoid bringing them out into the surf while also not losing them; not a big deal.

Neither of those things happened: what actually happened was, with the surf bliss-out and euphoria, I would paddle in, every single night, for maybe two weeks straight, and hit the showers. I would talk to the lads, and laugh and recount and gaze at the ocean and check out the evening tourist flow and whatever else. I would philosophise, and reflect – but one thing I would never, ever do was remember my keys.

Only, literally, at the front door would I remember: then, the cursing and the time bleed and the stashing of the board and the sprint – at night – back down to the beach in my short john wetsuit. And, I can say for sure, this didn't just happen once, but maybe, like, over a dozen times. Nothing could get the keys hard wired.

Surfers, a tae kwon do instructor had said to me in the pub one evening, are spacey. They go and surf, and they come back and try to work – but they are spaced out. But, hey, you know why she asked me? No, not because they are stoned. It is because, instead, they are dealing with such crazy, huge data when they surf: when to paddle; any sea creatures? How is the crowd? Which wave to choose, how many can I take – how deep can I sit and still make the wave? Which is the good one, how dark is it – am I lining myself up with shore?

Anyway, the only solace, when it came to the keys, was amusement: the lads would sometimes see me sprinting back and laugh outright and say, "Wow, look who forgot his keys again!" Eventually, that proved to be the solution: Zach would ask me if I had forgotten my keys, maybe halfway home, and I realised that I had. Eventually, something clicked, and I started remembering them – but it took a while.

Video Clips to Defy Zach

Zach, at times, was intolerable: I wasn't looking for credit or complements, but even the grudging acceptance of capability that other older surfers at Three's had eventually surrendered was lacking. Everything – every single thing – sometimes for weeks on end – was viewed negatively: even the good moments were laced with criticism and advice on ways to improve yet further. For sure, it was all good, and probably what I needed – to add a Hawaiian layer to many years of surfing in other places; the icing on the cake, the *piece de resistance*. But whatever it was, it wasn't easily earned, that was for sure. I would never be a North Shore hero, but I was getting somewhere.

Still, there had to be times when I pinned Zach back a little bit. Fortunately, the camera came to my rescue: a Surfline addition to the Outrigger Reef Hotel, it was, of course, a curse to any rational local. Hyping up the surf, bringing in the crowds, over- or under-selling it: every sin you could imagine. I cursed Surfline, I paid them: I checked and laughed at their reports every single day.

But the one thing they had was the camera: if you wore a watch, and could remember the time you got your best wave, the miracles of modern technology would let you rewind – maybe in the pub that evening – and watch yourself on your wave of the day. Sometimes it was chastening, other times a source of stoke:

it depended on how well you surfed, for sure, but was also a way to get yourself to maybe surf a little better.

Anyway, when the bombers came through, I was able to take it one step further by capturing stills, or clips. I was stoked: I was able to send shots of my best waves to the lads in Ireland, and whoever else might be interested. That included Zach: though form and style remained idiosyncratic, it wasn't too hard on the eye. Yes, for sure, I saw why Chuck and Zach had once quasi-affectionately called me The Mummy, but there were also good sides: fluid movements and styling trim, turns and late drops and hollow moments. And, above all, there was some evidence.

'Everyone is so Busy'

There was social commentary in the line up, as well: Everything got discussed, from Ukraine to assassinations to presidents to race riots to Covid, Covid, Covid. Vaccines, masks, restaurant polices – all of it got dissected and reviewed and critiqued, out the back, whether you wanted to hear about it or not. At least, though, there was always the metaphysical distance – always the detachment of surfers when discussing land affairs, as if they were some kind of alien race looking down on earthlings and finding them all so baffling, inconsistent, ridiculous.

Occasionally, moments of philosophy would emerge. Glenn was good at that. Because, maybe, there was, on any day – except the crazy days – also a sort of far-from-the-madding crowd feel: like anywhere in Hawaii, but particularly in Honolulu, and particularly in Waikiki, and maybe even more particularly in these parts of Waikiki, there was a major element of refuge in the ocean. Land had to be escaped from, occasionally – surfing was a good way, but, if I am honest, sometimes you even needed to escape from surfing – sometimes it was just going from one realm of humanity, into another.

Anyway, sometime towards the end of the pandemic, Glenn said that everyone, everything, felt so busy. It was true: it was one of those post-lockdown fluxes that we never really noticed at the time – but when bosses start cracking the whip, and looking at real or imagined, necessary or spurious, target or production goals – or whatever – and start the push-push-push vibe, and sort of stop telework, and move just beyond the boundaries of optimal health, to try and attain some kind of passé *beau ideal*.

I explained my theory to Glenn – explained why I thought everything was so busy – and he just sort of nodded, and said, "Maybe, maybe". He had seen a lot of more of Hawaii, and a bit more of life than I had, so I wasn't going to press my point: the fact remained that on some days Threes was, for sure, the escape route.

The Real Hawaii

Let's be honest: that is what I was doing. I was in a bubble, within a bubble – because, yeah, in US terms, Hawaii is a bubble. It is, in US terms, pretty much the promised land: some Americans dream of Paris, maybe, but most seem pretty dippy about Hawaii. Don't get me wrong: I saw my fair share of disgruntled tourists, and the graffiti on the curb across from my building said it all: "F*ck tourists, go home" – but, pretty much, the bubble of Waikiki and Honolulu – apart from the crazies and the druggies – pretty much seemed to deliver on everything. Shoots.

But the real Hawaii? Ho, bra. Well, one thing was it seemed like was that it would take money. A whole lot of spending money – but, even with that, not much could protect you from the driving, the traffic, the highways. From the commutes and the tensions and the competition for resources and the heat; from the prices of homes and apartments; from the sticker shock of the cost of living. From localism, violence, racism, reverse racism: from exploitation and resentment and capitalism and survival-of-the-fittest Darwinism. It was all there! It was a dream; it could also be a nightmare, that was for sure. But – by and large – yeah, it was a dream.

You could even see it, sometimes! Even from within the Saratoga bubble, yeah, it would creep in. Because that was part of the magic: fundamentally, there was something of the developing world in Hawaii – something loose, and unregulated, and very slightly feral – very slightly law of the jungle. You could walk to the beach across the zebra crossing, for sure – but there was no real guarantee, to be totally honest, that any car was going to stop for you.

And so many nuances: "There was this one guy", Mike's brother John, said to me one evening. "He was a judge. I was even up in front of him a couple of times. One day, out by Makaha, I seen him stop his car on the side of the road and start picking up pieces of broken glass off the road – he didn't know it was me, didn't know I had seen him. But from that day on I liked and respected him, for that – not for being a judge."

That was what to do. But there were times, for sure, when I realised the indelibility of my devotion to Ireland: times when I realised there was a Rubicon that I probably wouldn't ever cross in terms of naturalisation. Times when I watched the football highlights as Ireland played Armenia, or somewhere, and the Armenians got mouthy against the Irish and I shouted at the screen and said, with the greatest passion imaginable, 'Come on Ireland".

So Hawaii was a dream inside the bubble – and a dream and a beloved place if you were born there: a dream for the diverse, and for the rich, and for the locals, and for the tourists. But for sure, that left a lot of others – the fresh–off-the-boats, the less affluent mainlanders, and a lot of others – and sometimes, unless I played my cards right, me as well.

Because, maybe, the real Hawaii lurked over the hill, at the end of a sweaty commute – it existed in L & L's Hawaiian barbeque joints, and the big ethnic parties at Ala Moana Beach Park on the weekends – it existed in offbeat locales like Sand Island, and Waianae, and who knows where else. And it would, for me, for better or for worse, remain that way: I could never claim to have lived it, but I was aware of its existence and its impenetrability and its challenges – and maybe that was enough.

Local is Lekker

Local is lekker, they used to say in Cape Town: being local is what it is all about, in surfing and in life. Because, maybe, if you can't make it work on your local square mile, well, what is the point of getting in your car and driving a hundred miles – right? And the cool thing about this particular bubble, the Saratoga one, was that there was even a bit of country there – in the middle of town a big green space with plants, palm trees, and cool, cool other trees. Verdant, almost wild – amazing birds, and a lot of the country qualities. The sound of surf and the beach, day or night – there were plenty of magical, moonlit soirees on the beach, that was for sure – so why leave the square mile; why deal with all the traffic?

That was the stomping ground – I was never a local, and wouldn't try to claim it: but, for sure, there was a time when I was getting vaguely recognised. I was out there a lot, and getting lots of waves, but was still pretty sure no one knew me: but, from time to time, I would get a nod, or an introduction, or whatever, from someone who said they saw me out there all the time. 'That is a first!", said a South American lady to me one day as I paddled and missed one; I hadn't seen her before, but she said it in a nice way. "You are part of the place now", Mike said to me later. Maybe it was better not to be aware of it: I would probably have abused the status if I had really thought about it – right?

And, not to be too analytical about it all – but what is the dividend, anyway? What, for reals, is the point – yeah? I mean, you can become a local, for sure. Even in 21st century Hawaii, baby: you can put in the hard yards, and stick to a spot, and work your way up, and be there on all the good days and the bad days and the days in between. Not easy – but doable. You can greet people, get your face known, and take some verbal batteries, and learn the local rules of the road. You can eat humble pie and be patient and be audacious and wait and wait and wait and get bomber waves at the end of it all – once in a while. There are, for sure, upsides to being a local.

But is it what you think it is? What you imagined it to be? It is the vision – the dream? Of course not – mainly because nothing ever is. You can be a Three's local – you can surf there for fifty years, if you want. You can get like Chuck, and Dave, and Zach – you can get to the point where you hook the good ones, and no one really argues. You can reach, maybe, that moral crisis: you can get to that zone, like Gerry Lopez – everyone knows who Gerry Lopez is, right? – where, with uberlocal status, you actually end up feeling bad – actually end up apologising to everyone that you took waves from. Now that is a local, baby; that is success – the edgiest of double-edged swords.

But you know what? Only so many people even know you are a local. Beyond them, every tourist, every North Shore superstar, and every migrant ripper from the wave across the channel who only turns up when the swell is good – they don't know, and, worse, they don't even care. And when the circus is in full swing, there isn't a lot of time to tell people who you are, or where you come from, or how long you have been there. Basically, on those days, the locals have to scrap for their waves like anyone else.

Except, of course, for Chuck: the advantage of having a place dialled, of being devoted to it – if there is one – isn't in terms of relationships with people. No, no, no. It is in terms of relationships with the ocean. Chuck, who was in some ways the real local, the locals' local, was also a local to that stretch of ocean, reef, and wave. Not local just to society, but to the bottom contours, the oceanic rhythms, the patterns of swell, and a host of other variables, that had nothing to do with the human factor. That were related, if to anything, only to the surf – to knowing when the big sets were coming through, and knowing when the wide ones were coming in, and maybe even knowing a few other things as well.

Ireland for the Winter: Castles Clown

The Boat Harbour, Sligo.

Dodgy Return

After a little bit of Hawaii, expectations were high. Way too high: the absurdity of believing that there had been a quantum leap forward in my surfing was ruthlessly exposed, just hours after getting home. There, early in the morning, I felt like the Michelin man in my wetsuit – on an unfamiliar board, in murky water, on a wave that I had forgotten how to ride.

Surfing can be like that: a confidence game in which you question yourself, then others question you, and then the whole thing starts to unravel. Having gotten few waves, that Christmas morning, and looked stiff and cold when surfing them, I returned home despondent: it seemed like what had been the goal all along – to try to conquer not Hawaii, but Ireland, yet again – wasn't going to materialise. The time wasn't right; I hadn't been away long enough; I had been away too long: it wasn't yet written in the stars, or whatever.

But there were lessons for next time, for the next paddle out before I hit the road again: be humble. Get the right board. Be patient. Know that Hawaii had been a privilege, surf-wise, but that it wasn't necessarily going to translate – at least not overnight. Work the angles; get the right gear; stay healthy, and then maybe – just maybe – the years in Hawaii would lend something, not just to my surfing, but to Ireland as well. Wait, for the moment: wait for the wave that was going to break just right, over your shoulder, and channel all those moments of positioning, etiquette, awareness, patience, fitness, and finesse into that drop, that ride.

Castles Clown

At Castles, I was given another chance to show what Hawaii had done for me. Parking beside an empty white cottage in the usual grassy-muddy semi-legal roadside cove, which would have been unthinkable in America – even in Hawaii – we suited up, in the Wild West of Ireland, with a glimpse of the left point peeling down the rocks below. Indecisively – feeling the dynamic and importance and opportunity of the moment maybe a shade too much – I brought two boards, and thus two leashes, down to the break: across briars and stone walls and bog holes, I left one out of sight, resting on some thorn bushes, in case I felt like – or needed – a change.

I very soon would: almost immediately, after maybe my second wave, the makeshift leash fix that I had figured out at home a few days before – using resin and catalyst to get the plug to hold together – fell apart. The board got washed in, and so did I. No problem, apart from a bruised ego and a little bit – actually quite a lot – of time and energy and image gone astray. Who was this guy who had just been surfing Hawaii for a year, anyway?

Undeterred, I went in to switch boards; surely this was meant to be. I mean, who else man hauled two boards down to the coast on a winter's day, right? I had wanted to try out Newstalk's fish, as well; on some level, it was all working out pretty nicely. But things changed again, fast – as they so often do in surfing: this time, on my second-first wave, the leash broke, leading to a second, baffling paddle back into shore. I could see the black dots bobbing around in the line-up, asking themselves what I was playing at over there. The whole thing was getting, to be honest, vaguely comical.

Back to the rocks; back across the scree and shingle; back to the board with the still-functional leash, and a quick transfer of equipment for a last leash-board combination gamble: back down the rocks, back into the ocean, back into the changing tide, back to the increasingly ledging and critical left-hand point. At that stage, energy was becoming a back-of-the mind issue: overriding, it, big time, was the grim determination to hook a few. Sometimes, you need that in surfing: put the blinkers on, put the head down. Make it personal: not necessarily adversarial – but you are going, no matter what, to get some waves.

In the end, I did, but the episode ended in true style, fitting for the day, and a final resounding victory for nature – not to mention another chuckle echoing down from the Irish surf gods: I was, on my way back in, dragged across the rocks on the inside and bounced off the reef. Enough was enough: as I rose and gave an emphatic thumbs down to the watching lads, they laughed and laughed and laughed. Once again, the chance to parlay the island-style skills into Ireland had been presented to me; once again, the opportunity had passed.

Killers and the Frog Rock Paddle

The Slab, a mythical sort of spot, wasn't going to work. The lads knew it, but they were able to hook a few: willing to get knocked about a bit in the hunt for the one that stayed open. With the frustration that only the passenger can feel, I saw a way out: instead of watching from shore, or enduring a long and cold car park wait, I paddled back to Kilcummin.

It wasn't a big paddle, or a long one, but enough to make your imagination take flight: the waves rocking the shore; the cliffs overhead; the open ocean to your left. Seagulls arced and clouds scudded overhead: I guess people had done it before, for sure, though I had never heard that story – as a result it felt unique, and personal, and an exploration. A moment of binding with the land and sea and Irish coastline that was unexpected and offbeat; a story in itself. Maybe the spirit of Hawaii had made a difference, after all.

Hawaii 5-0: Sunset at Three's

Threes, firing.

Dings, Dings, Dings

One thing is for sure: Hawaii will make sure you pay the piper, one way or another. Oh yeah. I was getting so many dings, going through so many rites of passage, that eventually I started making a list. If I had stayed at home in Ireland, I might have gotten the occasional cut or bruise – totally – but this was on a completely different level. It was, I guess, a product of the time and the place – but I reckon that, it was, also, maybe a kind of island-imposed hazing – to see if you really wanted to live in the tropics as much as you thought you did.

Certain things, I was finding out, you have to go through in Hawaii: ant bites; jellyfish stings. Other kinds of stings, floating in the water; too much heat; adjusting to temperature. I got stung by a bee while I was swimming, one time: stepped on sea urchins many times, and got too much salt in my system from being in the water too long even more often. Got sun burned, for sure, in spite of best attempts, and in spite of hypervigilance – more superficially, I couldn't get my hair to look right, and had to keep it short just to stop myself overheating. I had sore knees and hips and shoulders and necks and whatever else, at one stage or another.

And there was more, much more: I bruised my ribs from too much lying on a surfboard; I developed super sensitive teeth from too much grapefruit juice. I got a stomach ache from eating local pears off the tree: I knocked my kneecap out on a prayer mat; I hyperextended the back of my knee; my nails acted up. I nailed my elbow and impinged my shoulder – I strained my neck from bad TV set-ups. I got sand stuck in my eyes, and even had a stye: my digestive system did cartwheels, and I needed magnesium or anti-histamines to rest in the intensity of the heat.

Playing cricket, I got eight stiches in my hand in between the webbing on my fingers. I got dry eyes at night from the ceiling fan; had to learn to rinse sinuses from bacteria in the water; cracked my lips, strained my lower back. My jaw went off-kilter and I pulled my hamstrings; I sprained a finger, and banged my surfboard on my head, and another day on my arm – leaving me with throbbing pain at night for a week. I got bad itches in far out places as a result of not understanding the local cleansing rituals; if it wasn't one thing, basically, it was another.

The list went on: dust in my throat from running along dusty beach paths; cuts from the reef. Maybe a little Covid thrown in – who knows, right? Ultra vivid dreams; sweating nights; occasional dehydration. Blurry eyes; sore kneecaps from days of uncountable numbers of small waves – a super shore shin cut from a collision with an apologetic lady; overstretched rhomboids from too much paddling. A karate chop with the wana when paddling in in the dark – boom, spines and stains and vinegar and, no joke, still sore months later.

What had also happened, I was sort of starting to realise was that Hawaii was, totally, for me, back to square one. In SF, in Ireland, I at least had the basics, right? Good diet, exercise, all that kind of thing. But I eventually figured out that that didn't just travel with you: It was, like, six months before I took a run again, and maybe a year until Zach helped me to get away from the processed foods that had infiltrated. All the balances disappeared: it was, to compare it to another football manager, a bit like Manchester United after Alex Ferguson: after twenty years, or whatever, of success – or at least something that defined an era – you move one part, and boom! The wheels fall off.

"Don't jinx it", Alden said when I told him I was just waiting to find out what the next injury would be. "Say you ain't going to get no more, and they will stop". And there were other ways in which it wasn't so bad, as well: I mean, how unlucky do you have to be to get injured? But, flip side, how lucky do you have to be to get injured only during flat spells?

And, also over on the flip side, a lot of long-term malaises got sorted out by Hawaii. For every ding it gave me, something bigger, and darker, could be said to have gone away: old habits of living, for sure. No more smoking, less drinking; changing patterns of relations with ambiguous influences in the Emerald Isle and California. A seriously painful twinge I got, for years, from surfing and soccer was sorted out by a spiritual physical therapist from the Philippines: everywhere, health advice abounded, from Reiki to naturopaths to osteopaths to everything else.

Diet improved; sleep lengthened and deepened; communications with nature augmented. Zach steered me away from processed food and towards water filters: the doctor, baffled by my saying I was 6′ 2″, measured me and said I was now 6′ 3″: maybe the barrage of health advice from Zach, and which pervades so much of Hawaiian life, and which focused at least in part on posture and alignment and balance, had made me stand up straighter. My hair and nails grew like wildfire – something was for sure, going on.

Transcending all of that was Hawaii itself: thanks to the Shoals of Time, and the tree in the park by the ocean – and thanks to the birds, and thanks to the sunlight radiating through the branches – all that developed into some serious siestas, as I would generally fall asleep after a few pages. The years of travel and wild nights, maybe, were being paid off in the grooviest possible way: the heat would put you to sleep, the sound of waves and nearby luaus and birds singing kept you there.

Difficulties with Dave

He's on a different path, said Skipper Dave about Dave. (I guess there are a lot of surfers called Dave; that not all surfers are called exotics names like Strider, or whatever.) Either way, anodyne as he sounded, he was a big presence in my life: from *bête noir* to heavy local, we probably spent more time thinking about each other than we would have liked. Like one always thinks about one's adversaries, we could not have been more different: his broad in the beam and beefy to my stringiness; his surly to my aloofness, maybe. But we were both there at the same times, on the same days, so there must have been some common ground.

And, hey, he was not even a bad guy! He wasn't even that bad of a surfer (as many older locals often are): "He is a good soul underneath it all", someone had said to me. But, on one of my first waves at Three's, I had paddled on the shoulder for a small one, causing a section to crumble. Pretty bad, sure, but no mortal sin: still, it was the wrong start with a long-term local, and after that, things went pretty quiet. Quiet, for, like, a year: that is the way surfing can be. You spend some of the best hours of your life – maybe more than with your family or your mates or your loved ones – with a motley crew of people you either like, don't like, or don't know. *C'est la vie.*

The big, big July swell changed all-that – sort of altered the–vibe – but nothing happens overnight: change had been coming for a while. I had talked to Chuck about the friction, and he gave me some advice, saying, basically, "wait". So I did, wondering what opportunity nature would throw up. And others had also left the question open: had also said that the smaller I get, the bigger he gets; Chuck had said that things would sort themselves out, for sure, but maybe there had to be some human agency in amidst all the mysticism, as well.

In a bizarre twist, it was a week of injury-dry-docked-ness, and switching to runs instead of water, that brought about some kind of catalyst. Dave motored into the line-up on a boat, so, to make things that little bit more challenging, there was none of the dynamic of chilling out and reflecting and untangling oceanic relationships like there was with the others. No chats at the showers, no talks under the stars: there seemed no way to overcome the impasse, therefore, until, jogging one day, I looked up from my runners and the pavement and there he was, loading up his board outside the Waikiki Yacht Club.

I pulled up and turned around and said wow, I had never expected to see you on dry lands: we talked, or I talked, and explained that things hadn't started right, and said why, and we sort of left it at that: agreeing to stay out of each other's way, and not necessarily to be matey all the time, and just left it at that. "You stay out of my way", he said, "and I'll stay out of yours".

And that, maybe, was good enough: not amazing, not perfect, not dreamy – but sort of ok, for now. And, anyway, the ocean, like Chuck said, always decides – not us! "Most people are OK above the high-water line", he said one evening – and the same could be said of the Kaiser's locals, who could eat you alive on the water but offer you some of their beach cooking in the parking lot. And so, yeah: it was funny that there would be sultry days, beautiful evenings; golden sunsets, when we both sat out there, Dave and I – sometimes on our own, never talking and still with that sort of Roald Dahl vibe in the air – but also vaguely interdependent, animal kingdom-style; vaguely (if it is even a word) sort of copasetic.

Big Swell Hype

A lot of things happen in Hawaii. Sure, not all of them are newsworthy, just because so much of it is ultra-local beach boy news – not the national, international kind. Simple things, nearby – like who is going to help to fix the local shower faucets; or why is there so much litter on the beach on a certain day; or who has Covid; or how often do the parking meters get checked? How many tourists are there; what is the traffic like – why is it raining? But, occasionally, local kine becomes news, and that is when the trouble usually starts – when it comes to surfing, that is.

The July swell was pushing a lot of buttons, that is for sure. Caldwell had seen it coming long before, but even he – usually pretty level headed, with along Wooly the Worm and Clarissa Catapilla – even he, it felt like, early in the week, was starting to go for broke as well. On Monday, the swell was anticipated as being the biggest since 1995 – a long, long way back to a pre-internet Kamehameha Day swell that, apparently, blew the doors off. But guess what? This one was going to be bigger.

It wasn't long before Surfline, and the media, and anyone who had an opinion, were in on the act as well. As the week went by, people in the street or in work might ask if you had heard that there were big waves coming. For sure, I had – but when? Slow onset was predicted for Friday evening, with bombers starting to come in overnight. Yet that is all anyone could agree on: the timing of when the swell would peak, or what it would actually look like – there was the tail end of a hurricane in play as well – or where it would break best, were all beyond the capacity of any forecaster – and way beyond me.

But, stepping back a little – what about a twenty-five-year swell, bombing in, the second season, anyway? Wasn't that sort of cool timing – wasn't that just right? Wasn't that the way that you might have scripted it – a year to get the eye in, then the year of the big swell – the biggest since 1995? Wasn't that sort of poetic? The fact that the swell was coming on a weekend added another layer of edginess: the whole week felt like a countdown, with emotions rising accordingly. A couple of times, I started to wonder if it were really even going to happen: could it really get that big? Could the south shore hold twenty-foot faces – would I be able for it? How many people would be out: how would I, or anyone, feel if it were too big to take on?

The only respite was from Chuck, who said it looked like there could be too much south in it. In itself, that gave me an edge in regards thinking about where to sit; on a deeper level, it cut right through, clean through that hype. Chuck had been around long enough – seen enough of the place and the wave – to know when to get excited. He stayed calm, so I chilled out.

Emotions Running High

As the swell hit, so too did emotions rise. And, yeah, the hype had been too much: on my first paddle out, I heard Big Bob, one of the Kaisers guys, a super daunting heavy, talking about how he had waited twenty-five years for that swell. Even though most later agreed that it was no better than the one in May, people seemed to have this idea in their heads that it was: that this was the one; the moment to prove and assert: that this was one, also, for locals – a time to beat chests, and make claims, and basically own the place for as long as the waves were coming in.

The funny part of it – if any of it can be called funny, which it sort of can, and it sort of can't – the funny part was that when I paddled passed Big Bob, one of the heaviest of the Kaiser's guys, he looked at me with intensity, and I said, paddling past, that he was Mooch's brother. And he said hi, how was I doing, and yet still had that same expression on his face: bewilderment amidst it all.

It took that swell to put some other things right into perspective, as well: on the biggest days, the gnarliest guys the south shore – maybe the whole island – could offer, descended on Threes. The older locals, like Dave and Chuck, had sent it all b–fore – but, on that one swell, the hyped swell, the once-in-a-generation swell, even they were surprised. The aggression, the invasion, the yapping, the sending-people-in: the vibe was way more than they wanted, needed, or liked.

So it was strange, when things escalated, to see Dave paddling back to his boat, and Chuck going in early: strange to see locals not coming out; strange to see even Zach paddling out super-extra-late. The locals – had been raided, pirated, and were of another generation anyway: all they wanted, most of the time, and as I saw that day, was to catch a few mellow waves in peace. But for all the pathos, for all the bathos, something had changed: no one owned the ocean, as every local surfer is quick to forget.

And, yeah, I hooked a few: watched for hazards, and fights, and all that – there were a few of each, those evenings – and watched for people in my inside, and people who took off late, and people who dropped in. (One of the Kaisers guys, in maybe the most enduring exchange in the water in Hawaii, had called some offender, some opponent, some miscreant – or maybe just someone who got in the way – a squirrel. A squirrel was, for sure, not a term of endearment: he said the guy was a squirrel shish kebab – said that he was going to smoke him like a squirrel, and sent him in.)

And so I watched, and waited, and hooked the wide ones – the big, wide ones, with Kimo's side bite fins allowing for a mid-face turn and the run and gun along the vast wall of water – that most people were out of position for. And turned on one of them, and saw Dustin from Rockpiles (Big Bob's son, no less) on my inside, and caught his eyes, and saw him shake his head, and didn't paddle for it – and, another time, saw him nod, and went. That was, pretty much, how it went.

One thing, after that swell, that I reckoned would be a good idea, no matter what, would be to get the hang of those Kaiser's guys – the ones, like Big Bob and Mooch and Dustin and whoever else – who hung out on a tiny corner of beach at the edge of the parking lot, near Rockpiles, and pretty much ruled that locale. And I did: on my runs, I would go past, and talk to them, and discuss the swell, or whatever. And we became, in a cagey way, sort of matey: I might, I reckoned, be, maybe, a fraction better off next time around.

Yakkety Yak (Don't Talk Back)

What happened next sort of had to be a product of the flat swell as well – after the big swell, and then three weeks of no waves, all sorts of things seemed to have changed around. When I paddled out on the second (and bigger) day of the next big swell, there were different faces, and Chuck and Dave weren't there. Maybe routines had changed, maybe people weren't ready to go back – who knows.

Anyway, with only Kyle sitting on the peak, there was a lot of room over on the shoulder for the wide ones often came through on a west swell. Feeling vibey on Kimo's latest board – my third, the V3, with these killer swirls and a little less volume in the nose, and a tail that looked like your thumb – I paddled out, and over, and waited – and even without the waves, it was a cool moment, for sure, as I had also just shaken off the latest round of injuries, and was feeling pretty good about everything.

From there, everything got a little better. A wide one came through that no on– saw – because, mainly, no one was lined up without Chuck there. Half an hour later, no one had decided to employ my same tactics, and it happened again: big and green and clean, Christina hooted from the shoulder and told me afterwards that it looked like a thing of beauty. Kyle said he wished he had sat wide when I got back out to the end of the lineup: Jon texted me later and said that I had gotten some bombers. Shoots.

Then, things got a little better again: the next day, the guy who had gotten the wave in front of me said a few nice words as well paddled back out: a shortboarder on the inside kicked his head back, as he sat on his board, and smiled, and mouthed the word "nice". Mauro texted me later and told me I had been charging, and that the waves I took off on were double overhead: on each of those bombers, I was shaking, literally, paddling back out. I hoped it wasn't visible, and tried, as best I could to maintain the same neutral expression, looking straight ahead – not making the mistake of looking around for plaudits, or recognition, that just might not be there.

After that, things got better, and worse, and a little gonzo: Hawaii was peaking out, and I was feeling my oats, and (by now the only one out the back) on the third day, a true bomber reared its head. It was dark and blue and looming, in that sneaker kind of way – in an intimidating kind of way. I was the only one far out enough, and so I turned and paddled and really, really wanted it.

The drop was big, feeling as big as a small building, or at least a garage: but I was too deep, behind the peak, and maybe me, or maybe my board, lacked an ounce of pace. I tried my best; had nowhere to turn; raced it for as long as I could, and faded in to the whitewater melee.

The tricky thing was, Zach was right there. Right, right there: right in front of me, just as I was engulfed. When I came up, already hurting badly within myself, Zach was already in full flight: ranting and raving about my awareness, and how I had nearly taken his head off. I knew, in my soul, that I had charged and had no option: he was sitting too far inside, that day, and my heart and my head for once agreed: I was right, I was right.

Let's not forget, I was also, like I said, amping: I told him to pipe–down – and might even have said a little more, and paddled off. I knew that wasn't going to be the end of it, but was at least hoping that there would be a little gap before we resumed hostilities. And there was, at the same time, the question of Felix.

Felix, a bald and pretty extreme older guy, had dropped in on me, totally faded me. maybe a year before. But he was the experienced campaigner, and I was the local rookie: he told me to show some respect, and paddled off, and we never spoke again. He was also mates with Dave, and boated in with him; I got the feeling that he was, for sure, a member of the opposition.

And maybe he was: but that day he wasn't – for about five minutes, anyway. Paddling back out after my beating, he turned and asked me if I made it, and I told him I made the drop but not the shoulder, and he smiled and said it was a hell of a wave. So at least I had that – right? Right until, out of the inside, Zach paddled by, still airing his grievances about our encounter – right in front of Felix.

What could I do? I mean, what would you do? Well, normally, like always, I would maybe bow out, and smile, and look the other way, and apologise, and tell myself that I was just lucky to be there. And, for sure, that was what I wanted to do this time as well: but because Felix was there, and because I was so stoked, and because of whatever else, I couldn't. But what would my cutting riposte be: what would come out of my mouth?

"Yakkety-yak", was my answer. "Yakkety yak, yakkety yak", I said to Zach: "Yap, yap, yap: stop your yapping". "Pipe down", I said: I said, literally, "Button it". I may even have said, in fact I can confirm that I did, highly adrenalised, "Come to Ireland, and surf like a man". Zach, momentarily speechless, could hardly believe his ears: apoplectic, he sat up on his board, and gave an old school fist pump gesture and splashed water over himself in his chagrin. He was, truly, in a flap.

All I could do, at that point – already feeling guilty and bad – was to dramatically change tack again, and say that it was a wind up: that I was winding him up deliberately, and that we were all good, and that I really was sorry – and that I was still smiling, though, and that I wasn't backing down, either.

Somehow, the cocktail worked: Zach laughed, and ranted in a lighter way: Felix, baffled by this double reverse kind of conversational dynamic, just looked curious and eventually paddled away. Honour on all sides had been preserved: the next day, as Felix was paddling in as I was paddling out, he threw me a shaka: Zach's rant hadn't changed the wave I had taken off on, and nothing ever would.

Outer Pops

By Thursday morning, events had escalated further. Still feeling sore from the night before, and jolted the presence of the excess evening crew, my solution was to paddle out in the morning – unprecedented, unheard of, and against every law of languor ever written. But this was, I was feeling more and more, a swell event – something that would be remembered; something whose absence would be felt in the ensuing days, and talked about for a long time afterwards. Go big or go home: go now, push the envelope, skip work, and concern yourself with the consequences further down the track. Or something like that.

But the morning session was a heartbreaker: having woken up early with the intensity of the swell (and associated behaviours) still ringing in my ears, I considered the early one – the dawnie – but my body said no. Hedging, compromising – always a bad move in surfing – I paddled out instead at nine-ish, into the teeth of a wild crowd.

There were not only the Kaisers guys, this time, but another elect as well: a caffeinated, guilty-because-I-should-maybe-be-in-work, kind of element. A morning crew that was as foreign as they were hungry: staring around me, I felt like I could have been in a different place. A different wave, country, setting: all of the familiarity of the evening surfers, which I now realised I had taken for granted, had evaporated. I was at the bottom rung of the ladder, and the rabid shortboarders had no time for concept shapes: before me, as I paddled for my only attempt at a set wave, instead of the crowd parting I saw only clean – or dirty – pairs of heels as everyone else prepared to roll the dice: to play chicken with each other, and the wave, as well.

With a mixture of resentment and liberation and hesitation and shame, I gave in: I paddled away. Over in the distance, I had seen, outer, outer Pops was breaking once in a while. A wave that Zach had occasionally, disparagingly told me to go and surf, I could never bring myself to do it: too soft, too friendly – too touristy. Today, though, things were different. Way, way outside, sets feathered in the wind, breaking indiscriminately and only rarely – breaking purely for the right surfer in the right place at the right time.

I wasn't that guy: instead, I sat outside of the pack and hoped that one would come my way. Anything to mark the occasion; anything to make skiving off work worthwhile – anything to offset the risk of sunburn. Anything, basically, to dodge the bullet of guilt and entitlement, that always comes with a waveless session.

None of that, unfortunately, happened: but something else, something better, transpired instead. What happened was that the wind dropped slightly, into a warm breeze: the sea felt different as I watched the circus at Three's from afar. There was then, all a sudden and out of nowhere, a bizarre sense of *déjà vu*: of fishing with my Dad in Ireland, twenty or thirty years before, on the open water; of sitting quietly, with not much happening. A sense of ease and tranquillity: a sense of the initial appeal of surfing, and of youth, and of load-shedding. A sense of tension dropping away: of space, of peace.

Gone was the competitiveness, the fevered rush and intensity of the last few days: surfing was, briefly, back in perspective. I paddled in feeling better than I had paddled out; paddled in with a sense, also, of having caught up with my Dad on some spiritual level. When I reached the shore, my muscles felt relaxed, my mind felt recharged, and I laughed to myself at the mania across the channel.

Zach's Lost Board

At least I wasn't alone: if I had been the only one to lose my board, it would have felt pretty bad. Fortunately – or no, unfortunately – just weeks before, Zach had lost his: surfing late at night, no leash, strong winds. The usual story, except with quite the twist: "It will turn up", he said. But despite such strained optimism, such positivity, he was, for sure, emotional: the board had been his companion for many years: it had surfed all over the island; it was something special. I wondered, for sure, if his certainty that it would turn up wasn't a kind of sadness, as well: an inability to accept that, yeah, maybe it wasn't coming back.

Anyway, it did: something like a week later, seven miles out to sea, it was picked up by a yacht. A needle in a haystack: a one in-a-million long shot. Yachts, I was learning, were good about reporting things like that – mainly because there was always the chance that there had, at one point, been a surfer attached to the board. Miraculously, the board got radioed in, and someone heard about it, and someone else told Zach.

There was more to it than just getting his board back, though: there was a kind of sense of luck as well, a voodoo vibe. Zach had, somehow, been vindicated: the ocean was on his side: he was lucky; things were going his way. He was being rewarded, it felt like – and he was going to be sure to ride that particular karma wave, as well.

Sorting It with Daniel

The irony, and the absurdity, was that – on the next swell – as I wound Francois up, and as Daniel wound himself up, and as Zach pushed his chest out and backed me, and as the rest of the lineup watched or looked away – some really, really nice waves rolled through. Maybe half a dozen, unridden: all sacrificed, or overlooked, for what had happened over a not-so-great wide one that everyone happened to want.

Today, we are all mates: François and I talk about rugby; Daniel calls me Sea Bass – or, even better, the Sea Monster. But, that day, it was just one of those situations: one of those moments where your heart rate goes up, maybe, a little bit; and fight or flight (or fawn or freeze) instincts take over; and time sort of slows down: a moment when the passage of time is, Einstein-style, slightly affected. And it's always more intense in the ocean, anyway – always trickier when in a different country, and when not even really that close to shore. When you are half a mile, or a third of a mile out, you feel differently about confrontation, and conflict – about the proverbial swinging of handbags.

And, maybe, even more fundamentally – now that I am thinking about it – it was one of those sort of 'self' moments: who are you, anyway? Believe me, I was no kind of tough guy, least of all in the Hawaiian surf: but I had the Irish flag on my boards: I had some kind of thing, clearly, that I wanted to represent – and it wasn't always just smiling and laughing and drinking and joking; not always just playing the Wild Rover, or the Plastic Paddy.

It wasn't the first time that sort of this went down, and it wasn't the last: with Dave, there were a couple of flash points, where I also felt that same shock, followed by recoil, followed by apology, followed by maybe a little bit of topspin on the apology to keep them guessing – followed by explaining who I was, and that I was pretty far from home and on my own, and that we sort of did things differently in Ireland – but, surprisingly, that our way was not necessarily worse than their way…

Anyway, sorry! Sorry, sorry, sorry: here is what had happened: Daniel, who I guess had been nursing a few justifiable grievances, had been winding me up: leaving the nose of his board trailing in front of me as I was taking off; maybe not moving out of the way with what one might call alacrity but dinged his head on his board after I had chatted to him, coincidentally, maybe a year or so before. There were, probably, other things as well: that little bit of wave greed, maybe, on my part: that little bit of my excessive paddling and that little bit too much of my kid-in-a-candy-store focus on number of waves per session, in the early days, rather than other things – rather than bigger pictures.

So, back to the day in question: so, yeah, I kept getting waves – and thought I had yet another one, and looked around, and there was François, the French guy. And I was like, "no worries", and took off anyway, because Zach was shouting at me to go for it, and I knew I could kick out pretty fast, and it would have still rubbed Francois' eye a little bit – all ok, only there was this one lady floating on a longboard – a deer in the headlights – and I had to run over the nose of her board to get out. Cool, but not that cool.

Faced with a pretty demand from Daniel (who really had nothing to do with the situation, but was for sure watching what was going down) to go and apologise and offer to pay for her ding repair, my Irish self, for sure, reared up. But there was another side to it: even though she was wrong, she was a lady, and she was clearly embarrassed, herself, by her transgression of paddling in front of a surfer on the wave. And Daniel was playing the *beau sabreur*, and leveraging the pathos, and maybe he was right, and you sort of had to respect that. Still, it was ever-so-slightly humiliating, for pretty much everyone: maybe, because he was younger, I should have told him to piss off and let it escalate. But by this stage, either way, it wasn't cool – put it that way.

And so I thought fast: I paddled to her, saw how spooked she was, and said some nice things – right in front of everyone. Compliant, remorseful, apologetic, confessing. And then, pretty much, after maybe thirty seconds, maybe a minute – just paddled back out – stopping for a chat with Francois the protagonist on the way, whistling La Marseillaise – and stopping to go eye to eye and rail to rail with Daniel for a moment, and had a few words – and paddled away. After that, I reckoned I had Daniel figured out now, and it wasn't in a bad way: he saw himself, maybe rightly, as an equaliser, as a freedom fighter – and, yeah, maybe he was.

The Flat Spells

These are the times that try men's souls, brah: the days on end when no surf comes through. Sure, you could saddle up and drive and face traffic and parking and locals and maybe find a wave somewhere else: you could risk getting your bike stolen – if you had one, which I didn't – and risk sharks and thorns through your flip flops at Diamond Head, or Sand Island. You could watch, watch, watch the forecasts; you could pray for surf, and you could swim and snorkel and run and rest: but there was no easy cure for the flat spells, that was for sure. "No more nothing" Mike would say, half questioning, half stating: no more surf, nothing left. Nothing, nothing, nothing: flatness, the great Pacific lake. The double emphasis: not just no more, not just nothing.... But both!

For whatever reason, the second south swell season in Hawaii was just that: a flat spell, punctuated, every few weeks, by macking, long distance, long interval, sublime, crowded, powerful swells. That was the way it was some years, I guess: something to do with la Nina, or el Nino, or climate change, or whatever else. Sometimes, in between, according to the forecasters there would be some Tahitian wind swell, or trade wrap, or a SOUO, which was pretty cool. But my life, just then, was pretty much dominated by whatever kind of radical and nasty-sounding winter storm was bombing off the coast of New Zealand, and which way it was tracking – and all that kind of thing.

That was cool, when it was happening, up to a point – but your body gets burned out, and your mind does too, after too many days of solid swell. So when it wasn't happening, that was cool as well – a time to repair, rejuvenate, relax, do other things. A time not to worry about whether you could sprint out of work in time to make the evening session: a time to pretty much be a normal human, with all those kind of vulnerabilities, for a while.

But those same flat spells, after a while, could grind your soul down, mate. Hawaii was surf-central – and if you surfed well you were royalty – but surfing had a flip side: you had to stick with it, even when it wasn't –here – mainly because, being a surfer, you probably had no Plan B set up anyway. You had to live through repetitive, quiet days; you had to keep hanging in there, and not drink too much, and keep your head, and try not to wish you–were – just for a little while – somewhere else.

Maybe they were good, those flat spells: without them, nothing would get done, most likely, and surfers would probably be even more far out than they already are. Maybe they forced self-examination, and got you off the merry-go-round, and stopped you thinking only in terms of weather forecast horizons for a while: maybe they gave you time to write down your stories, and take a look in the mirror.

Big Fish

And, yes, even that happened. Let's not dwell on it, not make a big thing of it: let's, sort of, just pass over it, for now. One time there was a black tip; another time we were out there, and one surfaced, and sank – and it wasn't that big, but it made a splash, and some people got spooked. Chuck, who wasn't out, and who had never had any kind of issue after forty-five years of surfing there, write it off as a passing Galapagos, or something. He could even joke about it: "One of those? Out here? In the ocean?"

No Angel

Let me be honest, as well – just in case it wasn't super, super clear already: I was, for sure, no angel myself. No, no, no: *au contraire, mon frère*. Not bad in a bad way: not a fighter or an insulter or a stink eye-er: none of that. But, for–sure – and pretty much anyone I ever surfed with will back me up on this – no angel either.

There are angels out there, for sure: people with those temperaments that stay super chill, even in the ocean – even in the surf. Even in crowds and on bad days, they will just let it all wash over them: I used to think I was one, and maybe I once was. Maybe it has to do with getting better at surfing, and more into it: maybe standards change – and as you elevate up the pantheon, or ladder, or whatever, it all sort of closes in on you: responsibility, experience, refinement, sensitivity: entitlement.

But, like I said, I wasn't all that bad. And, I will say this one thing: the badness, when it came out, wasn't ever, ever aimed at the people who were splashing and smiling and just having fun. Well, hardly ever: sure, occasionally there was a need to say, "Hey – that was sort of dangerous!", or something like that. But I had been tuned so many times in my life just like–that – and had felt it so intensely at the–time – that I was never going to be the one dishing it out to the foam board riders.

But the surfers that were bigger than me, badder than me or – if it is possible – more selfish than me? Well, that was sort of different. Don't get me wrong, I wasn't sizing up to any huge, tattooed locals – though they, any time I surfed, were always the friendliest. No – it was reserved for certain times, places, when those even more entitled than myself wanted more than they deserved.

I could get mouthy: I called Zach a squirrel, more than once, when things were tense. Yikes! I told Dave off, and used to ask Skipper Dave how many waves he had gotten that day if it seemed like he was overdoing it: I could also, for sure get super, super greedy myself and take more than my fair share of waves. I could cut inside and use all the other dark arts: I could, for sure, be no angel, sometimes.

But, this isn't a confessional or a request for forgiveness: I am not proud of it, but there is a way, in surfing, that all that is part of the script. Part of the paradigm, part of being human, part of life in the ocean – part of the way there are no rules in surfing, really, apart from prison rules or playground rules. And, in a way, it was what you needed to do to survive: the bigger ones take from you, and you take from the ones below, but you also push back against the bigger ones – or some kind of jungle, Darwinian law.

I was also, obviously, Irish: the ancient fires would come out sometimes, and that was, also, just the way it was. Maybe if I were Nordic, or British, it would have been different: but there is passion in the Irish veins, and it manifests itself in tricky ways, sometimes. To have done nothing at such times – to have been passive, to have been an angel – would, sometimes, have been worse. Strange, but true.

But you know what? There was a better way, a more effective way, a cleaner way, and it is this: get better at surfing. Change your board, change your diet. Stay fit; do exercise to offset your weaknesses. Because skilled surfers, literally, surf across and over all of that: they run the numbers, and get their waves, and avoid all friction, and then paddle in.

Bad Times Out to Sea

And amidst it all, even with all the beauty and the nature and the surf, you could feel embarrassed about being out there at Threes. On rare days, when the stars were misaligned, you could feel bad about the indulgence and overgrown kid aspect: about floating around like a waterborne monk, and about other things that I could and would – and, yeah, maybe even should – have been doing, if you hadn't been there. For sure, it would get to you sometimes: when conversation, maybe, turned in a certain existential direction. Or when you felt like you, or others, had been out there too often – and you maybe saw yourself reflected in them.

But, for sure, there was only one day when it really, really kicked in: a hyped swell that was small – and, worse than small: super, super lully. Everyone and their brother and their sister was out there, turned on and tuned in by misplaced surf reports: everyone waited, and the night got dark, and people got edgy and made horrible grimacing faces as they paddled for waves. I caught maybe one, and felt – truly – embarrassed to be there: as bad as when, years before, I had neglected my sister's visit to South Africa to surf a wave called Farmer Burgers – leaving her and her boyfriend on the backing, mosquito coast. Bad, bad, bad: some nights, it is true, you are better off not surfing.

I guess, probably, that fed into what happened next, when the swell really did come up: maybe things got a little dramatic, a little intense. Maybe, as well, things aren't quite that well defined. Like I said to Zach and Chuck afterwards – I am no angel myself, that is for sure. But there were thugs out there as well, same as anywhere.

And, well, yeah – it had all been building up for a while. There can be clashes of characters in the lineup: every time I felt that, though, I remembered a time I had paddled right past someone, and was reminded of the adage that the weaknesses we see in others are the ones we most hate in ourselves – or words to that effect. 'Don't let it escalate", said Doug – 'Who are you to cast any stones", said Zach. Yes, for–sure – but there is a limit, right? I mean, are you expected just to check every value you have at the door – just because you are in a new place? Is that how it works?

Anyway: already incensed by a little bit of a snake move by one of them, It wasn't easy – you have to pick your battles, that is for sure. I mean, he wasn't some kind of six-foot muscled tattooed madman who it would have been certain death to confront – that would just have been insane. But he wasn't small, either.

So one day, with a lot going on in terms of mounting tensions, and all that, I paddled over to one of them as he was paddling out, and, as the South Africans say, I tuned him a little bit. I may, in a moment of passion – a moment of sort of exploding – even have told him that he was a disgrace to surfing, and good luck to him, and that he should, maybe, watch out for his own karma.

And that was all that happened. But why did it happen? And why did it happen then? Was Zach part of the problem – could I blame Zach? Had I taken too much of his sledging when it could, and maybe should, have been distributed a bit more evenly across the line up? Were there people he was daunted by, and who he didn't want to confront – and was all that spilling out on to me?

Maybe, maybe – but probably not. Sure, maybe that was part of it – or was it that, for some unknown reason, thanks to some unknown trigger, things had boiled over? Was it because I had started reading *Papillon* again – reading about life in the penal colonies of French Guiana, and how you had to be smart and tough and lucky to survive in them – and had been thinking of how totally like surfing that all was?

Either way, I didn't expect anything good to come of it: regretted it pretty soon after I had said it. But what I hadn't figured out, maybe, was that semi-ungoverned element of surfing: the way that it is, in some way, jailhouse (or, come to think of it, playground) rules. The way you had to think a little bit about Papillon, again: that some people would only respect resistance;

that they would only change if you turned, and pushed back, and went from being the hunted to the hunter.

Not my cup of tea, and not all peace and love, and maybe I lost a spiritual battle that day – but, yeah, it was what it was. "Just say it anyway", Darren a helicopter pilot, said to me once, when we were talking about what to say, and when to say it, and to who. –Sure – those people", he said, "may be brick walls – may laugh at you, ignore you – but they will remember it that night when they are going to bed, as well."

Break Time

The thing was, though – and not at all to dramatise it, in any way – but, yeah, something slightly, very slightly, changed after that. Just a fraction of an angle, just a *soupcon,* but maybe it was enough: the total perspective vortex that I had fallen –n to – the world of self-created drama, as Zach called it – the Three's rabbit–hole – fell away: just a little bit. The idolisation and perceived irreplaceability of the Utopia of the spot was maybe shaken by it all – probably in a good way. Because wasn't this now one of those situations where you are getting too far from what surfing is meant to be about – one of those times when you realise you are paddling out (or, worse, paddling back in) filled with frustration, and bad energy – and all of that?

"It is just water", said Chuck, seeing my distress. "This wave is like a drug, but a really bad one: where you get a quick jolt but then want more and more". But, hey, he was out there as well – and swiftly stroked into the wave of the evening. How did that work, my inner surf-Gollum asked?

So, the next few nights, just to rein myself in, I surfed at Paradise, and it was, in a way, exactly that: paradise. Because, you know, guess–what – there are other waves! Other places! Other people and crews and opportunities; other tropics, and cold places, that might bring just as much to the table as that special – most special – of waves could. Three's was the best wave, maybe, but not the only wave: right across the channel, Paradise – some days – could give it a run for its money.

So, yeah, maybe there was a line in the sand; a Rubicon; a tipping point: Three's was no longer, after all that drama, maybe, worth sacrificing it all for. I mean, exploding at someone was also an example – the ep–tome – of that, right? The moment when you are like, "Well, I sort of have to back myself on this one issue – even if it puts the wave, or getting the best waves on any given day, in second place." When, also, it is not worth just sucking it up all the time: not worth trading off waves against pretty much everything else.

With all that, also, there were other dimensions: any way I sliced it, it was a spiritual battle that I just wasn't winning. I mean, when there were no crowds, there was no problem: everyone lived in harmony. So were certain surfers the problem – or was it the blow-ins? Was it the lack of a real bruiser, a real heavy, in the lineup? And –as I – perish the thought – part of the whole problem?

So, yeah, overall it was probably healthy to step back. And – who knows – maybe it even helped: I guess you have to show a little back bone, a little bit of an edge, when it comes to confrontation. Maybe fight is better than flight, is better than freeze, is better than fawn: maybe life and surfing is a combination or a cocktail of all of the above. Maybe, also – because it is so unregulated – surfing requires a bit of the Wild West mentality, now and again.

And maybe there was even more to it than that, now that I come to think about it: because the weird thing was, actually, the sort of irony of it all – the absurdity. Because, after maybe five minutes of reflection, I realised there was no way to win in those situations – I mean, what if my dreams came true; what if – purely theoretically – all those guys who were getting under my skin, and up my nose, had stopped turning up?

The reality was, I as tried to envision it, that it wouldn't be such a good thing: that it might, in fact, even be a bad thing. That it would be a pyrrhic victory, a hollow victory, and a victory with lots of strings attached: that word would spread that now I was puffing my chest out too much – or whatever other way you wanted to frame it– But – worst of all – what would have happened is what always happens: I would, in a sort of Kafka way, turn, or morph, in to one of them.

That is what happens – right? That is what happens in revolutions: the idealist turns into the dictator, the communist into the control freak – all of that kind of thing. Things get lost, and you think you have changed things – but it is a *plus ca change* thing, in reality.

And (most likely, just around then) there were other factors in play, as well. I had to find a way to chill out at Three's. I mean, I had to mix it up somehow: had to work within my boundaries. Because, for sure, I had boundaries: to the North, the Ala Wai canal; to the West, the statue of the owl at Kewalos at the end of my run. To the East, the view of the surf from Diamond Head, beyond the cricket pitch: to the south, Three's.

Within my corral, had everything that could have happened, happened? Chuck didn't think so – though his standards, were, to say the least, pretty high: after two years, he said there had been, maybe, a couple of waves that were eights. But, he did say that anyone – even him – could get jaded after seeing big swells roll through.

Was, as Tom had said to me, there an actual limit when you had seen a lot, if not all, of what the wave had to offer? The incidents and accidents, the hints and allegations: the bathos and the pathos and the highs and the lows? Was it like Jürgen Klopp – another football manager – who ran his teams so hard that he never got a third season out of them? Eventually, even the cam rewinds lost their lustre: why didn't I care if I didn't look back and see myself on a good wave anymore? And why were some surfers – pretty harmless ones, starting to get under my skin: were they really taking to many waves, or was I just sort of going overboard on the whole thing?

And so I kept paddling to Paradise – even though I wound up at Three's, each time, later: kept paddling across the channel to try to get my headspace right, and burn some energy, and return in a different way. But, even with all that, maybe it all boiled down to the same thing – the ocean, and the unwinnability of it all, and the mutability of ourselves in that context, and all that kind of bird's eye view. I mean, the ocean – it just sucks it all up, and absorbs it, right? That is its great strength: it takes away our stress, but it also works both ways: it just doesn't care about these spats. They aren't part of its history; they just fade in to the deep blue.

The Reunion

For about five minutes, it was, seriously, all peace and love. After three weeks of no waves, one day it ended: the forerunners came in late on a Friday night, and I was out there with Skipper Dave to get some before the crowd – as wave-starved as we all were – inevitably hit it. I stayed out late, soaking it in, and trying to get some rhythm back in time for the waves to come.

And people were stoked to see each other again: were paddling up and saying hi; were exchanging stories about where else they had surfed, what else they had done. Pretty soon, naturally, things got back to normal – with everyone scrapping over waves and behaving pretty badly – but there was, briefly, a magical vibe of elation and reunion and tolerance: of handshakes and fist bumps and sun shining and waves coming through.

This one flat spell was sort of a big deal on a number of levels. First, it went on for so, so long – right at that time of year when the waves should, by rights, have been pu-ping – that it felt like it was never, ever going to end. I mean, one week – ok, good. Two weeks – sure: beneficial; injuries healing; starting to think about other things; benign realities. Planning for the future – that kind of thing. But three weeks and beyond – well, in Hawaii, which is the most surf-centric place on the planet, things were likely to get a little frayed: a little edgy, maybe.

Obviously, in some ways, it was a good thing. It was reminder that you better not put all your eggs in the surfing basket – and, even if you did, you might end up jaded and super selective, or slowing down physically, or whatever other self-limiting factors kick in with any form of monomania. A reminder of the trade offs: that surfing was like a beautiful lady who only turned up every now and again, rather than someone you could really rely on, right? Or some kind of related analogy – but, any way you sliced it, things got rough after a certain point.

The days melted into each other; the forecasts, even the long-term ones, never showed a hint of swell. The sun beat down, and I swam and ran and snorkelled and hiked: tried to plug the gaps left by the lack of waves in any other way possible. It was a time to write about surfing, rather than riding waves: as Andy Martin put it, writing comes after the fall, when there is pretty much nothing else to do.

On the Road with Zach and Igor

Surf trips, anywhere in the world, have an element of the bizarro to them. They wouldn't be surf trips if they didn't: I mean, for sure, you can probably try to put together a sanitised, organised, non-gonzo surf trip if you really try – maybe it has been achieved. But, in my experience, the list of x-factors always outweighs any kind of day-to-day balances of probabilities, or predictabilities.

Hawaii was no exception: with a fellow Euro from work, the first trips took us on to military bases where should-have-been-here-yesterday semi-private waves rolled though. The set-ups weren't great, but people got a kick out of the privacy: I am sure those waves had their day, just never when I was there. More significantly, though, was the context of the blind leading the blind: John was new to Hawaii and there were, as he adjusted to US driving, numerous instances of Italianate lane changes and panicked alterations of direction.

We got waves, for sure, and John was a cool guy, but when we were leaving the west coast at a so-so, not-as-good-as-Three's, wave called Rest Camp and I realised, when we pulled in to the petrol station, that I had left my phone on the roof of the car – only to find it was still there – I reckoned I had used up too many of my nine lives. It was time, maybe, for some more local motion – if I could find it.

With the greatest Wahine of them all, things looked up a little bit: spending the night at Malekahana beach, on the windward side, in damp and mosquitoed cabins, any discomfort was more than made up for by the sound of falling asleep to the ocean and campfires. More than compensated for, as well, via cool little waves that rolled through into a small corner of the headland: waves which broke through frames of palm trees, into aquamarine water.

Still, maybe there was even more to it than that – but, on the other hand, maybe there wasn't. Missioning to Makapu'u for a beach clean up with Zach and Igor, I tapped in to the old indomitable-Gaul thrill of the surf mission: three men in a car, just totally owning it. Griping and laughing and telling in-jokes and critiquing; turning up the music, the lads telling stories of each surf spot that we passed. This, I reckoned, was cool: this was just like the old days.

When we got there to find that the clean-up was on the other side of the island, we weren't deterred: on the baking sands, small bodysurf waves were breaking, and we all got our fair share of womps below the brooding cliffs. And there was, throughout, that surf trip sense of invincibility and super-power: we were in our element, and pretty much just owning it.

Things got a little out of whack, for sure, when Zach has to stop for a fairly lengthy bit of personal banking; they were restored by a visit to a shrine for a lifeguard they had both known, and even further by some kind of SF-style overpriced brunch. The trip to Wal-Mart that Zach tacked on the other end, with the noble goal of getting me a water purifier, was too much, though: seeking my usual post-prandial rest, I was instead inserted into a pretty competitive and overcrowded parking and shopping arena. I tried to explain that I could get it all online, these days, but no go: he was a man on a mission, and it was a classic surf trip kidnap – but he meant well, and no doubt I am healthier as a result.

Vampire Nights with Mauro

I knew Mauro from the surf, from the town. A good guy – super good. So solid. Fit and hungry and also humble – and yes, he did look very, very slightly like a vampire. But it was more the names

– Zachary, Mauro, Sebastian; Ireland, California, Venezuela – that leant, at least to me, the ephemeral, briefly-mustered, after-dark crew its romantic allure.

We would sit out way, way late. It isn't a good thing to do, and not to be recommended – but wow, we got waves. The best waves, empty waves – big waves, sometimes. Seeing the shore light reflect on the surface, sometimes in the moonlight – feeling the curl of the wave, and just about making each other out. Actually, because of the back lighting, I think it was actually easier to see others riding than to see the way oneself – it was hard to see the waves and ocean contours shorewards, but there was an amazing sort of beige-pink-blue backlit element to the sets breaking outside.

Other times, even more ethereally, when it was super dark – no moon, cloudy – there would be these moments when it was impossible to tell if the wave, or your body, or the board, was even moving. On those kind of glassy, still nights, all frames of reference would disappear, Einstein-style – until you saw the curl forming beside your head, and realised – amidst the ultra dark, and the ultra white nose – that you were moving like a bat out of hell.

'Why you always surf so late?", Mike asked one evening. And it was true, – did – and yeah, it was a good question to ask, and one that truly needed to be answered: why? Was it the sun? Was it the people, the need for space – those twenty minutes into twilight when everyone was surfed out and there was a chance to hook the bombers?

We would watch for each other, dodge each other, but above all support each other. It would have been pretty much way too extreme for anyone to be out there solo at that time of night – but, because others would go, you could as well. A sort of surfing socialism, maybe – in direct contrast to the greed, accumulation, and quasi-capitalism that seemed to surround the surf just an hour earlier. And there was, for sure, the benefit of us seeing each other: "That wave was your height, and another one of you on top", said Mauro one evening in his deep accent. and I could not have been more stoked.

Gyrating Against the Wall

Sometimes, just to pass the time, things got really far out: at the showers, Zach, working himself up into a lather, would break down every detail of my stance and show me what he felt like could be even further refined. I was into it, for as long as I could either keep my cool or keep a straight–face – but sometimes, for sure, he really, really pushed it: one evening, particularly excited about some political issue, he strode up to me at the showers.

"Get over here," he said, referring to the adjacent bathroom walls. Without further ado, he told me to line myself up in parallel with them: together, like some kind of bizarre prog rock act, we got in to surfing stances and swivelled hips, knees, shoulders – rocking back and forth, as Zach tried to explain his interpretation of how to find the best speed line on the wave; how to distribute weight through the body; and how to position oneself on the board.

Hey, I am sure it was good for me Zach had a way of surfing that, no joke, channelled yoga and some kind of body-consciousness into every movement: I was stoked to learn. But, right then, it was evening, pretty dark, and, as always, there were lots of tourists around. Tourists always get a kick out of surfers; you generally get a nod and a close examination as they walk past: to many of them, surfers, I guess, might represent pretty exotic creatures. But this, for sure, was on a whole other level: as they sat at the tables eating their sunset dinner, or herded sandy kids towards the showers, you could feel their eyes – their bafflement and bewilderment and possibly their disgust – at such bizarreness. Inwardly, I laughed: tomorrow they would be gone, but we would still be here.

Chuck's Lost Board

Everyone lost boards: everyone was human. A lot of people, for so many reasons, didn't wear leashes: it was vanity, skill, tradition, ease, comfort, expertise, experience. It was a thing – a scene, a vibe, and a badge of honour. Cords, or goon cords, or whatever you wanted to call them, could still get pretty badly stigmatised: calf leashes were, ok, I guess – but if you really, really knew what you were doing, you didn't wear one.

I got it dialled, after some effort, and saw the benefits: only the increasingly nocturnal nature of my surfing, and the intensity of the crowds, and the serious sadness that involved the loss of my first board, kept me from not wearing one more often. Plus, sometimes I liked to get off the board and swim and tow it a little bit, stretching out my neck, so it made sense. At least to me: screw the vanity and the kudos – at least for now.

Chuck, on the other hand, never wore a leash – only on the big days, maybe, when he described it as a kind of social responsibility: there were days when the waves and the crowd would put even the most expert, even the most experienced, in situations where they have to decide to let a board go – maybe at speed, through no fault of their own, and maybe in the direction of another surfer, maybe a kid. That gnarliness was lessened, a little bit, by a leash.

And, yes, losing boards when surfing with no leash could happen to anyone – even to Chuck. When he lost his green Brewer on a mysto trip to Sand Island, I was asked to put the word out to Kimo, who shaped over there – and to the beach boys, who I saw every day. That one never came back, and when he lost the yellow one on an August swell, well, that had to be a sign: twice in two months was too much.

That second time, here is how it went down: it was a good day, the waves were firing, and Chuck was getting a lot of them – a lot of the best ones. Maybe, possibly, just a little more frequently than normal: his sixth sense was firing, and he was on point for anything and everything of quality that came through. He was the master and the maestro – and had every right to it, even if, sometimes, I badly wanted the ones he was on. Like a vice-president, for a lot of it was I second in line, which, on a one-wave set, is nowhere.

Anyway, he lost his board: word filtered out to me and Zach and Mauro as night set in. We heard no more, so presumed he had found it, but surfed on with one eye out for it – but it was getting super dark: a true needle in a haystack situation, if it was even still out there. And so we rotated and scored and hooted and congratulated each other: this was our time of the evening, the vampyros, and surfing came first. And then, out of nowhere, Mauro kicked out of a wave and shouted that he had seen Chucks' board right beside him – in the channel, in the darkness, as it was floating out to sea.

There was a very strong general feeling of stoke: Mauro paddled Chuck's board in, and towed his own, which was cool of him (and would have been very tricky if Mauro hadn't been wearing a leash), and Zach and I got a few more. Part of me, though, wanted to see what went down on the beach: Chuck, presumably, had been fretting by the showers, as anyone would have been in that situation.

Actually, he hadn't been: he had, like me and Zach, gone through the horrible, gnarly moment when you realise you are swimming far from shore in the dark, and you need to think about yourself instead of your board. That random point when self-preservation takes over, and you have to swim in: Chuck had gone through all-that – but had seen Christina on the beach, and borrowed her board, and paddled back out to search. It was all pretty chaotic, pretty intense, by local standards.

Anyway, as Mauro and I got closer to shore, I shouted to the fishermen, – who, from the blinking of their torches were in the know as–well – that Mauro had found the board. And Chuck was paddling back in by that stage, or heard me shout, so we all pretty much reached the beach together, in the dark.

And that, pretty much, was it: Mauro floated the board to Chuck, and Chuck went up to Mauro and shook his hand, big style, and gave him a proper, proper hug – right there in the water, right by the shore. Mauro is low key, and Chuck is reserved, so the moment only lasted for a second – but there was emotion and gratitude and stoke, all mixed up, right there.

Chuck loved that board, the yellow one, way more than any other: afterwards, by the showers, we all processed and sort of celebrated and talked of other things, as you do when something sort of sensational has just happened. And that is it: the next day, Chuck appeared with a leash, which he didn't want to talk about, and surfed – with me and Zach and Mauro – until way after dark.

Sunset at Three's

Why did we always surf at sunset? And what was it like? Ok, I'll tell you: it wasn't as hot, for one thing. You weren't going to get fried, or bake your eyes from staring at the sun; you weren't going to damage your skin, or your vision, or end up having to wear sunglasses in the water. You would avoid wind; see the same people over and over; and be with a crowd that had, maybe, had its edges rubbed off by the end of the day.

The dawn patrol, I had heard, were a mellow bunch of old schoolers: I saw one paddleboarder, Clarence, who had a huge handlebar moustache, parked up across the road from me, most days. Then – and this part I could say "yeah, for sure, totally" to – there was the slightly gnarly nine a.m. crew. There was an edge there; I mean, what sort of great or terrible life lets you surf regularly at nine in the morning, right? And so on, throughout the day: different crews at different times, reflecting different demographics; lifestyles; personal philosophies; physiologies.

For me, I had, usually, finally physically loosened up by the end of the day: finally gotten kinks out of muscles. And there, was for, sure, the magnificence of the sunset itself: the trippy changes in shading of Diamond Head; the sunsets and the green flashes and the orange ball of flame and the way it inched into the water, each evening: the days work done, dues paid, and good night Honolulu.

And the way, also, the moon rose and the waves glassed off: the way you saw the occasional shooting star; the way the sun moved in and out of the mountain skyline as it set, according to the time of year. The tourist boats passing by, down the channel, bringing their last customers back in; the solo captains sailing back out, to dock elsewhere, as darkness set in.

And, ultimately, the way the crowd faded out, and you had to train your eyes to the–dark – the way that the waves might pick up a little when you were on your own, and you had your choice; and the way the wave faces changed from green to blue to dark blue to black.

Better and Better

Progress? Yeah, there was. I am not going to lie: there was a lot, lot, lot. It was like being a kid again, that feeling of progression, though I guess this was now all details and refinements: this was all to do with learning the subtleties. I mean, did you know there is such a thing as popping too fast? Or that you can jam the tail out on a turn by thinking of karate kicks? Or that it is way, way cooler (but also way, way harder than you think) to let your hamstrings relax, and legs lengthen, when paddling? Or that you have to use your hips as much as you can when surfing?

And what about changing the board sitting position to fix your lower back; what about the subtleties of getting to hollow sections – going lower and, briefly, slower, to hook them? The idea of pushing down, or fading, into the corner of the wave for speed: getting your exhales right when popping, and letting waves of energy move through your body. Polishing the bottom of the board for smoother take offs; looking around at the lay of the inner line up the way a cricket batsman would survey the field. Putting weight on the front quadrant of the board for fast sections; perfecting the prone out: by that stage, for sure, God (and the Devil) was in the details.

And one thing about those small days – those super clean, empty days, towards the end of the year, when the south swells had backed off, and so had the crowds – was that you had hours, literally, to refine your style. To perfect your prone outs: to get more and more in to balance and stance and posture, and every one of the thousands of details that make up surfing.

Did you know that if you tilt your left shoulder forward when you are paddling for a small wave, it makes all your take off movements easier? That it pulls your front foot into the right position, effortlessly? You didn't know that? Well, neither did I. And did you know, as well, that the ideal prone-out involves a little shuffle – a spring backwards of your legs, and a sort of wave of lying down on the board? No? Hey, same here.

The small days would be relentless, as well: you would get off, and paddle back out, and there would be another one – right there, in front of you. And you wouldn't want to miss it, in case there might not be another one for a while, but – boom! Another one would come, and you would be doing that, over and over, all day: paddle, take off, surf, kick out, and paddle back out, pivot, go again. Sometimes, not even sitting on your board: one time, not getting my hair wet until maybe the seventh wave.

Oceanic Karma

Does it even really exist? Is it a thing? Is it way, way too open to interpretation, and is it just a way to pick on people: "Wow, he had some bad luck, he must have been really bad – his karma, from this or prior lifetimes – he must have been so bad…" You know? What is with the whole karma thing? It seems, a lot of the time, like a double-edged sword: a foolish and deluded England football manager once said that people with disabilities were being punished for past sins….. Whatever, mate. (He lost his job soon after.)

So it isn't a great place to go, I guess – although, as John Lennon said, maybe there is something like karma, even if it isn't instant, that can creep up and grab you. And with the huge, huge frustrations that could accumulate in the lineup, I asked Chuck, one day – in an unrelated conversation – what to do about frustrating people, and situations, for example. "Leave it", he said. "The ocean will sort it out".

Well, ok. He said some other things as well, for sure, but that was the takeaway: wait, wait, wait. And (maybe) hope, hope, hope: not for punishment or bad things to happen to people – though that was tempting, sometimes – but, instead, for time and the ocean to judge. Leave it to nature; see what happens.

And I can say, for sure, it happened to me. Injuries followed greed; bad vibes followed bad behaviour. In Hawaii, things moved pretty fast in that regard – like pretty much whatever you threw out there would boomerang back, big time. And it happened in other ways, too: Zach and Chuck got maybe too confident; they lost their boards. Skipper Dave got too greedy and took a board to the–head – Dave got sciatica after a radical run of wave hunting and gathering. So, yeah, it happened: it was real. If you had been bad, you had to watch your back.

The Paddle to Clarence's Party

SUPs, while totally uncool, could for sure keep you sane at flat times. I went out to turtle canyon and tangled with the dodgy boat operators who thought they owned the place; I used it to snorkel pretty far out, and made it as far as the Elks Club one time.

It was also a new form of transport: Clarence, one of the HCC lads from Zimbabwe, was having an African gathering over on Magic Island. I had for sure done some time in Africa, so was stoked to be invited: arriving with my paddleboard under m– arm – getting there past Kaisers and Bowls and the Ala Wai channel and in through one of the lagoons – I felt like my horizons had been expanded. I had a new way of getting around, and didn't have to worry about parking, or crashing, or traffic, or insurance – or anything.

But the way back, maybe, was a little more difficult. Going across the Ala Wai in the dark, in particular, was a far-out experiment: I guess the fish were not used to having people paddle by at that time of night, and I guess I startled them, big time: in the blackness, they splashed, and a couple even slid across the board. There was, for sure, a sense of alarm: this was no time to be disturbing their tranquillity, their privacy. I was later told by fishermen that some pretty big fish hung out there at night: when I told Zach what I had done, he just laughed, and said not to do it again.

The Gentleman's Hour

It was, for sure, a thing of beauty: after all the hassles and the vibes and the whatever else of the evening sessions, daytime felt good. Sure, it was sunny: sure, you had to walk between the raindrops in work, a bit. But it was empty, a lot of the time: one surfer, pretty punky looking, told me he called it the gentleman's hour – a time when you could for sure let others have waves, and not stress about it all, and just wait for the next one, and just generally chill out.

So you turn all the nighttime into the day, and get double sessions in, and have really, really chill evening sessions as a result – but the problem was, it killed you: weekends were a shambles of exhaustion and recovery. Work was edgy. But I knew the story of the Italian soccer writer who wrote a book on a team, and lived there, and everyone liked him – until he got too into the whole thing, and started shaking the tree, and was basically frozen out after that. So, yeah: I knew that going too deep was horribly uncool; that I had to get away from the evening sessions for a while – or at least turn up to them in a different, more exhausted way. "So that is what you have been up to", said Chuck, seeing me one afternoon.

They were hard to navigate, that was for–sure – those daytime sessions, that usually turned into double sessions: everything came down to rest and diet and survival-level work, while everything else fell apart. And the time – wow. Shoots. Time zapped, flashed by: the click had not been made that could measure water time at Three's. It was one, and then you look at your watch, and it was two: four or five-hour days in the water; they sure made you sleep at night. But to skip meeting up with mates? Was that going too far? Or was that just the way it was, in Hawaii?

There were times, for sure, when I wasn't sure if I should go, and had to ask for guidance from the universe, or whatever – but I generally got away with it, pretty much. And, though it was bad, it was also very, very good for me: not just in terms of defusing the evening tensions, and keeping me out of trouble – but also, maybe, in terms of old deficits: in terms of righting the record on days gone by when I didn't surf, and should have.

And surfing, *qua* surfing? The way people said it was just a drain; no return; nothing to show for it except maybe physical fitness? Yes, for sure, those doubt could shine through: you could see, in Hawaii, many a cautionary tale of surfing, and surfers, gone wrong: Mike said to me once that that was where it all went off the rails – Garrett, a dentist, said that his parents had warned him that surfing would turn his brain into a hardboiled egg.

But is it really like that? The way I was seeing, it, surfing had no real shape, no real evidence: if anything, it was a kind of benign blob in my–life – blue and shiny and changing shape, but benign: something, as well, with many downstream effects that never got measured, either. Sure, it was a time eater: sure, it led to paranoia and stress and it could be expensive and unreliable. Sure, sure, sure: but there was, really, nothing better.

The Moon in the Wave

Of course, naturally, things got a little unusual sometimes – like they always do with surfing, right? Those moments where you are sort of thinking to yourself "wow, this just wouldn't happen in a soccer match" – but to think it started from a poison oak rash in California? Well, that was, for me, a pretty major leap of the imagination.

The flight back to Hawaii was ok, actually – sure, my skin was starting to look a little off from the hike the day before – but, for sure, it was no big deal. It really kicked in the night after I got back, though, when there was constant itching and no rest – one of those nocturnal sorts of things. The next day, I was like, "ok, time to get this sorted", but I didn't want to really make a big thing of it – so reckoned I would see how the next night went.

The next night was worse, that is for sure, and I was pretty fa–t, the next morning, in checking in with the doctor. No prob, said the doc – here is a full-on steroid injection in your bum; enjoy; and go and get these pills, they will sort it out. No worries, nice one,

I reckoned – and even said yes to a flu shot while I was picking up the medications. And it didn't stop there – getting back to the Pagoda, the manager, Chris, when she heard my story, insisted on giving me a patch – some kind of stem cell activation patch, that you wear at the top of your spine. So there I was – patched, double jabbed, medicated, and pretty much ready to go surfing.

It was only when I was stashing my keys, that evening, that I started to feel maybe a little lightheaded, a little giddy – wondering, actually, if it was such a good idea to surf right now. But there were waves, and I was feeling good, maybe a little too good, and so I paddled out and chatted to the lads – maybe a little more lyrically that I usually would; maybe a little less aloof.

And also, in case I forgot to mention it, it was a full moon. (At one point, I kept track of all the far-out elements of my life that happened on full moons, in Hawaii, around that time: In January, the noise from the street was out of control: in February, I had intense conversations with mates under a palm tree. In March, I moved house; in April, the blood moon rose, and my body acted up. By May, I felt better; in June I surfed that wild night with Zach and Cunningham. In July, I had late night intoxication – in August, I was super tired. Always the full moon drama, always the full moon memories.

But tonight was different in other ways, as well: the full moon came up early, and stared radiating down on to the surf: on wave after wave, as it got dark, the moon split in to a thousand small moons on the face of the wave, and shimmered and glittered as you surfed – passed underneath your feet, and lit up the lip of the wave right along its crest: formed a moonlight carpet that the board glided over, and exposed the intricacies of the curling face.

Back at the showers, Zach and Skipper Dave were laughing at my unwonted loquacity: I told him that I had literally surfed on the moon, but didn't mention the cocktail of pharmaceuticals coursing through my system that had, maybe, enhanced the experience.

Ireland for the Winter: Through the Green Door

Tenth wave at Killers.

Bitten by the Shamrock

Drama, drama, drama: everywhere, drama. I mean, when do you get to draw breath? Form the Zach frying pan into an Irish fire: in to the bigger, badder debate on Irish secret spots; the deep, deep undercurrents about the secretive Irish nature – dating back, maybe, all the way to the War of Irish Independence – rebelling against the need, possibly, for the country to showcase its resources on the world stage. And there was dealing with the Irish winter itself, and dealing with ding repairs to a board that Kimo had shaped for Ireland and that had – no joke – been run over by a baggage truck on the runway.

But what was really happening, though – what was really happening to me – was Ireland. You can't say a country is out to get you, right? I mean, I love Ireland, and I hope it loves me back: it is a country shaped like a teddy bear, after all. And, yeah, I know Ireland – in some abstract way – loves me. I know it doesn't want to kill me. But, yeah, sometimes it felt like that, that was for sure: sometimes, it felt like that expression, which, goes, I think, "kicked from pillar to post".

Because there was nowhere to hide: I nearly cried in the airport, no joke. A freezing grey rain fell: my phone wasn't working. I had no euros, and couldn't get the ATM to work: all the bus timetables were now online. I couldn't call anyone, and, to be totally honest, I am not actually sure how it all came together: but it did, somehow I had forgotten to switch something off airplane mode, and after that it all came together. Just in time: my board bag was ripping; old injuries were hurting.

Ireland, after all, is – for real – the crucible: it can be the hardest of the hard, and it will, no question, put you through your paces. You can keep your SAS, and your Delta Force, and your Special Forces, and your mafia: put them up against an Irish gypsy, and they have no chance. And so – in sort of the same way, after the same kind of battles – after a couple of weeks, good things happened: for the first time, I thought about mana in Ireland. I felt a little better tuned in to Irish nature than I had before – and, as well, what was coming as sort of a shock to me was my wave riding curve: I had not planned on being a better surfer than ten years before.

Through the Green Door

There was a full moon as we set out. Back to being the surf car factotum: back to checking traffic and reading forecasts and doing whatever. Back to shooting the breeze in the morning darkness: Newstalk was a happy-go-lucky bag of cheery paradoxes; he could pretend to sport right wing views, sometimes, but would always then contradict himself. He could be impatient – almost military – but wore a ponytail: he was blue collar, white collar. He was also a big and muscley man who surfed small boards, and a coffee drinker, and a hell driver, and seemingly some kind of robot: his job with the county let him take days off seemingly any time to chase surf with little notice – and his surfmobile was, by my standards, palatably comfortable.

But, was that it? Was there more? Maybe, yeah, if you really want to go down that–road – to get–deep – maybe there was a bit more. Maybe it was comforting, amazing, cool, that we had dialled the trips in in such a way, that we knew each other so well by now, that the routine was now level, predictable. Maybe, though, it was a plateau, right? Maybe that was bad, or maybe it was good: maybe things had settled – calmed, or something.

Foamo, who we linked up with on the Sligo shore, also had a long hair surfer sort of vibe, and had recently moved to Easkey. He had lived in California, worked in the film business, and loved his tripods: he shaped boards, but only ever surfed foamies, as far as I could see. But he had made them an art form: he surfed MR twin fin models; he researched fins and waxing options, and just loved the whole scene.

So, there we were: three of us, having driven around and check a few spots, standing on the shore at the righthander: the three of us, sizing it up, and wondering what the vibe was with the big, shifty, too-short-interval-but-clean-and-lined-up waves: wondering if it was just on the right side of makeable, because the sun was out, and there were surfers out, even though no one was catching much – and because, mainly, there was no other show in town, so it was pretty much go out, or go home.

Irish surf standards, by the way, are high: high, high, high. Irish surfers charge, are fearless, and don't, most of the time, even know it – that is the beauty of it, maybe. I know it, and realised it then: not just because of Hawaii, and comparisons, but because of what I was seeing, and what I was feeling, as I went way, way down the shore to paddle out – and arrived, a little while later in the lineup: knew it, because I saw the lads laughing, and joking, while big, bad waves came through.

And that, though, was it: I didn't get any waves. After all-that – after the board, and the travel, and more travel, and the preparations, and everything: after the months of dreaming of it all: no waves. It was that kind of dawn patrol: wrong mindset, wetsuit felt wrong, board didn't feel floaty enough. Wrong position, got clipped a few times, lost belief, wanted to leave: that kind of thing. One set pulled my leash so hard that my calf hurt: no matter what, I decided, I was out of there– and – after maybe half an hour or an–hour – started the long, long paddle to the pier, and a slippy seaweed walk, and some serious reflection in the Irish winter sun.

And so I stood there, again, with the lads, feeling naked, even though I was wrapped in neoprene, and thought about packing it all in, and thought: what happens now? Newstalk, who had apparently gotten a good one, wasn't helping with his reminiscences: was he winding me up; rubbing it in; or fuelling the flames? Trying to get me into some kind of raging bull, over-the-falls mentality? –What – and not to sound like a paranoid surfer, because all surfers are sort of paranoid – was his game?

Two encounters, looking back, showed the merest cracks of light: I met with a ding repair man ("That's your man", said Foamo, nodding at his van), who told me he could fix the board, and Rosie, in the pottery shop, said shew was selling my surf books. By the time we reached Foamo's gaff and drank tea, things – maybe – were turning a corner.

And, yeah, they sort of had to: the mission, no doubt, were getting strained. We had missed a right point earlier because the wind and swell were wrong, so we tracked back to check it, adding on miles and time – and I knew I was the reason, and I knew I was the one who was getting sulky; which sort of made it all worse. And then we tracked back again, which made it even worse again: and then Newstalk said we were, no doubt, getting in at a wave he called Green Door, and I called the Boat Harbour, because he had seen a hawk flying over head, and took it as a good omen.

Ok: I was into the hawk but, even though I was grasping at straws by that stage. But, deep down, I was sort of annoyed at the way he called it Green Door. Yes, sure, there was a house with a green door on the side of the road: yeah, it was sort of a cool name for an Irish wave. But the wave had been there before the door, right? Had been there before it was painted green? Or was I, maybe, getting too caught up in the details, in my sulk, as I vowed never to call it Green Door, and always call it the Boat Harbour? (A few hours later, I would be re-thinking that).

So was there a pivot? Maybe: maybe there was, on the shores of the Boat Harbour, after the lows of Easkey: did I say a prayer, right then, to the Kevany ancestors? Did I do that? Because, right then, everything hinged, everything pivoted on getting it right: on having fun, on winning through. And, you know, I think I did: we were standing right in the heartland of my grandparents, and their parents: right there, for hundreds of years, in that exact spot. I had tracked it down on past visits, and, yeah, maybe imagined, occasionally, that I felt a vibe from the land.

I'm not saying the prayer was answered, or anything: but that is when it pivoted, if it ever did. Maybe that was when Ireland opened the door again, just a fraction, and came in to focus: when

I picked my way across yet more treacherous rocks, caught a ride in the current, and arrived to the right hander. Yeah – maybe it was then.

One thing was for sure: it was all about the line up markers. From the lineup, there was a handy boulder that I could see on the shore and which lined up with two telegraph poles behind it – and a lateral one, of another pole, over the arch of a house. (Later, at Inch, it was all about two buildings on the hillside, and the way the one ended where the lower one began – and about a dip in the hill to my right, and another house that would be right in the middle of it at the right moment. At Kilcummin, everything rotated around the eaves of a yellow cottage and – further north – to the way to other houses stacked on top of each other.)

Anyway! Anyway, anyway, anyway: the main thing was that the Irish water – the Atlantic – was grey, but not just grey. It was grey and super, super cold. And it was grey, cold, and opaque: you couldn't see through it. And it was something else, beyond grey and opaque and super cold: it was physically heavy, like liquid lead.

And surfing, in those situations, I have come to learn – much more in those situations than sunny warm ones, though the same thing applies – is about choices. It is, really, all about choices: all about emotional, cerebral, visceral, intuitive, counter-intuitive choices. I mean – right then, right –here – there was one, right? There was the choice to paddle out, the choice to sit there: the choice to talk or not to talk – the choice to see it as fun, or life-alteringly spiritual. The choice to take off on a certain wave – and the choice, in this case the choice of choices – about the inside section.

The Boat Harbour, I knew from way before, could be so fun, so forgiving, so beautiful. All of those elements were there, no doubt, in the take off and the early part of the wave: but all of that disappeared, on this day – on this swell, and on this–tide – when the wave reached the inside section. There, you could see from a long way away, you were going to have to hit the gas: no time for turning or playing: no showmanship, or showboating, or posing, or anything. There, the wave hit a slab of reef, and reared and raced – and went, almost, faster than your surfboard.

So – right there, right in front of me – the choice: dice? Gamble? Have a go? Risk the reef? Well, ok, yeah: let's try it. Let's be overwhelmed by the speed and shape and hollo–ness – and run and gun down the line, and go twice as fast and twice as far, and see what happens. And let's get out of it, by the skin of the teeth, and sort of flop into the water, still burning speed, and look around, and feel super stoked, and paddle back out. That, pretty much, is what happened: that was the choice. And after–that – after that introduction – things just got bigger, and better, and faster, as tide, and mindset, and belief, and the whole vibe, evolved.

As time went by, and the swell pulsed, the bigger ones broke wider, so the boulder marker became super critical in the river mouth current: you could see it moving fast, even when you were dead –till – and paddling was not, unfortunately something you could really stop doing for long. But as the session went on such diligence, such hyper vigilance, was rewarded: as time went by – as you learned how often, and when, the bigger, wider ones would come through – bigger as in, maybe, head and a half – you could, in theory and in practice, be in the right place, at the right time.

And so I was through the green door: because surfing is about known unknowns, right? Or is it unknown knowns? For the latter, you know the possible results, but don't know which one you will get – right? For the former, well, that's also a part of it: because there are always x-factors on any racetrack inside reef: contingencies and experiences that you could not have foreseen. Through the green door, into the unknown unknowns: through the green door, and back into Ireland, and stoke, and good vibes, and all the gnarliness of the damaged board – and the cold, and the hectic return from Hawaii – fading, fading, fading.

Like always, one wave stood out: like always, there was one that defined it all, and it went like this: the take off, the turn, the easy part, and the sprint. And then, the inside, and a sort of growing section, and the hollow curl of the wave above my head and over my shoulder and slightly ahead of me – and the colours: the blacks on the greys and greens; the whites; the ripples on the textured face, reflecting and shadowing light – and the noise: the plunging, draining sort of noise, like being down a plug hole or something.

Other things had happened, as well, in between: I had opted to stay quiet around the three other surfers, but wasn't sure if that had sat so well: one guy, Redbeard, was paddling back out right in my take-off line a few times – and, yeah, maybe I hadn't been polite enough. Even then, there was bizarre humour: fading Newstalk and pulling out and letting him have it, I cursed the thing and laughed as the others disapproved, for sure, of my naughty brinksmanship. The irony being that Newstalk didn't mind, and he the victim: such are the complex, hidden dynamics of Irish surf lineups, I guess.

In the old days, those sort of local Irish surfers were, for me, as cool as it got: they were the ones you wanted to be in–with – to laugh with, to joke and smile and nod and shoot the breeze. Discuss the weather, the tides, the waves, anything: I was, pretty much, a pretty good, pretty normal kid – always the one trying to chat them up. The flipside was that – sometimes, not always – they weren't so receptive, yeah?

But now that flip had flipped, that was for sure: Now, after two years in Hawaii pretty much on my own, I had, maybe, developed a certain way of being – a certain way of hanging back, and chilling out, and speaking when spoken to, and nods and expressions and eye movements and hand jive – all that, for sure, I had learned, covered a lot. But now, back in Ireland, it didn't seem to work – now the local lads were offended, maybe, by my lack of repartee: now they wanted the jocular, the jokey. It was twenty years too late, but that is cool – it was nice to know.

Anyway, soon it was just me and Redbeard out there: after a while, he said to me his first words of the session: "Looks like it has turned off". Was this acceptance, friendship, respect? Was this me and him – the last two who had seen it through? Maybe,

maybe not: either way, we paddled in, in the wind and the rain – a grind, against the current – and into the early evening gloaming; the twilight; the blue hour.

There, the serious business of loading boards and getting changed and staying warm: the time when the analysis, reflection, and even stoke itself had to be put on hold, a little bit. Only when changed, and loaded, and getting the news that Foamo's car ignition was on the blink, and that there was a bit of a situation to be dealt with, did the mood change from one of survival to external awareness.

And so we all drove back, and he made some calls, and we heard later – while reliving the session in the car on the way home – that it was all good with his car. I felt like saying to him that in the west, in the winter, you need a bulletproof pick up, or something – but then remembered my white shoes as I got out of the car that morning, into a muddy puddle, and him saying: "You're a brave man wearing them around here".

Crucified in Kerry

At Inch, I could say for sure, you couldn't have gotten a cigarette paper between heaven and hell: they were right there beside each other, those two p–aces – cheek and jowl. Rubbing shoulders, sharing the air, scratching each other's backs: batting me back and forth between them – toying with me, and reminding me, for sure, how wild the universe really is.

In San Diego, myself and a mate called Richie, to illustrate the point a little more, had played a gamer called lackey – hackey sack with a lighter – in the dog days of beachside summers. We would sit – or lie, or stand – on other sides of the room: using only ever the back of our hands, we would flick the lighter at each other, only catching it, as well, on the back of our hands. It was quite the skill: we could do twists, pivots, no-eyes, and behind-the-head moves after just a few weeks.

This time, though, I was the lighter: flicked back and forth by the hands of–fate – but first, we had to get there: first, we had to leave super early, but not early enough for Newstalk: when four in the morning was proposed, in the dead of the Irish winter, I had to say I was going to hang back. In hibernation mode already, nothing felt more unhealthy: he relented, and let me sleep until six, or a little before six, which was, almost, good enough.

By now, the missions had formed a rhythm of their own: I would push for more chilled approaches, and he would take endurance – his and mine – to the edge as a result: it was, in that way, a pretty functional game of performance-enhancing cat and mouse, centering around what petrol stations to stop in; what waves to check; and squeezing out amusement where we could find it – usually in short supply when it is still dark on an Irish winter morning, gunlining it across the country. He was, maybe, the terrier, the Jack Russell, straining ahead, gunning to go: was I maybe the leash? And was it the universe, higher powers, holding the leash? Who knew: we were warm, and well fed, and the boards were still on the roof, and the rest of the world was working – and that, pretty much, was enough.

But, still, there was no playing around. No, no, no: through Adare and Farrenfort and wherever else, each town just a marker on the road to the goal – by which time, on arrival, there wasn't much in the way of sightseeing, either. Not much more, to be honest, that a roadside check in the wind and the rain, and the call made to get in, and a hike to a nearby field to get a view from high–r up – and a struggle into the wetsuits, and some selfies, and into the sea – nearly, that is – because I was, for sure, even slower than usual.

It gets like that, right? I mean, we had just been moving at the speed of light across the country an– now – to–ally – the vibe, the instinct, was to hold the pace: so Newstalk was in to his wetsuit and waxed up while I, naturally, was still sort of contemplating the infinite: taking a few drinks of water, and just sort of getting to grips, slowly, in a cagey sort of way, with the situation.

And at Inch, there was, for sure, a lot of inching going on: I wasn't, no way, going to break or sprain or strain or cut something. No way, no way, no way. And so I inched, inched, inched down the hillside: I was going so slow that even my leash periodically getting stuck on rocks, and making me backtrack, felt like a minor delay. That, seriously, is how slow I was. Inched across the rocks, bum first – and inched, inched, inched to the water's edge, stuck right in that zone where there is, no question, no option but to go forward: no option but to somehow, impossibly, find a way over and around and across and through gaps in the jagged coastal rocks – and, finally, frayed and frazzled, into the water.

After that, though, there wasn't a whole lot of inching: after that, it was all about the paddle, and the current, and the inside break – and some pretty tricky, sort of traumatic, duck diving. All that, combined with some other things: with early morning tiredness being washed away, and hits of unwelcome adrenaline, and cold immersion – and, for sure, some pretty deep thoughts about surfing, and what was it all about, anyway?

And, – yeah – what about those waves, anyway? What about those right handers, half a mile long: lined up, stacked, steaming into the bay? What can you say? Why were we doing this; why were we there? Well, maybe because, walking along, a lot of the time you can see a wall or a hedge and think, hey, I surfed a wave that big. And sometimes you'll see a ceiling – and be like, hey, I surfed some bigger waves that were that high. But Inch, now, in the dark grey morning, was on a slightly different level: I look up at trees – really small ones, saplings, but still trees – and think of those waves. And I look at a picture of Eddie dropping in at Waimea on a poster on my wall, and, though they were smaller, yeah – I think of those waves. There is even a name for it, as there is for everything in surfing: 'double overhead plus'.

And, yeah, they could bite: they had teeth. For sure, they would start detonating pretty far away, close to the cliffs, and you could sit in the channel and be safe – most of the time, anyway, until the really wide, really big ones streamed through once in a while – and there was, literally, nothing to do but dive for the bottom and hope your leash didn't break.

And there were other moving parts, as–well – that is for sure: a devil's wind on the face, creating bone-shuddering cross chop, and holding you up in the lip if it wanted to. But – but, but, but

– when you negotiated all that, here is what happened: you got a view, past the wave, of distant mountains and beach. You hung on with your toenails inside your booties, and you made the drop. And you faded, a little, and looked out and saw a sort of greyish-brownish tint on the wave, with maybe a little golden element there as well – just a hint, nothing big, nothing dramatic – maybe from some stray little bit of sunshine that had gotten through.

Then, after that – once you had processed all that, and sort of gotten your bearings – a few other things happened: the wave would rear up, sort of like a horse on its hind legs, and grow a little bigger. But it would also make you cut back to get down the next step, and then you would turn again, and might get a little bit of a smooth face because of some kind of wave-wind-sheltering thing going on – and then, right about then, you would look up.

And what would you see? You would see, no doubt, a big, big wave. A wave that was both below you and above you: a towering crest; not malign, not nasty – manageable, but definitely towering. It was, for sure, a majestic sight: it was, no doubt, pretty much breathtaking. And if it didn't swat you – which it could – you would ride, and ride, and ride, along the point and down the reef and in to the cove and along the cliffs, and kick out wondering where you were, and turn, and see – way, way back, up the point – a couple of black specks that marked the other surfers sitting right where you had just come from.

It was all, in a way, too much: after a while, Newstalk said he was heading in, after I had seen him on some good–ones – saying he was going to climb back up the cliff, and would meet me on the beach. Ok, sure, sure. No worries: go for it. But then a few other things happened: the one thing being that he took–ages – ages – to get a wave in. He had, that day, a bad case of a bad thing in surfing: a bad, bad case of last-wave-itis, which means you aren't going anywhere until you get a good one, whether you have had a great session and want one more, or whether you have had a terrible session and want the golden moment that makes it all worthwhile.

So I was hanging back, not rushing, but also trying to do the maths: I wasn't going back up the cliff, no way, and I wasn't waiting on the beach – and I sort of wanted him to take some pictures from the cliff, if I am being honest. But, also, I was getting cold, and getting tired, and the waves were getting bigger, and – guess what: yes, you guessed it – everyone else had gone in, and I was bobbing around all on my own.

That, alone, is sort of a big thing – you have to, or I have to, sort of switch gears: whenever that happens, a lot of the Dutch courage – the laddish courage, the Irish courage, the Kodak courage, just evaporates, and you have to think again about the risks, the rewards, and all of that. Wave selection becomes a bit more conservative: everything is less good, for sure, but I guess there is always a chance that someone is watching the heroics from the coast, right?

Well, yeah, maybe – sort of yes and sort of no, at least on this occasion. Hey, I have no doubt that there were a few onlookers as I hooked some late, great ones: solo surfers always have a little bit of a romantic cachet, right? But one thing was for sure: I could feel a lot of eyes-on, on that paddle back home: from the moment that I knew it was over, and that I had to start paddling against the current, against the tide, and through the shorebreak to the beach, I just got this feeling – and here's to the good people of Inch – that there were a few people keeping an eye out, looking through their windows, just in case.

Because, it was a long, long, long paddle: it was an epic paddle. It was a lot of strokes, that is for sure: at one point I was counting up to a hundred to see how far I got, but that got so, so boring, and it only got me a fraction of the way. My beloved lineup markers now changed angles only incrementally: I was moving, but it was snail territory, and there was a long, long way to go.

Anyway, good news: I made it. I got though the shorebreak, I got to the beach, I survived: I pointed my hands to the sky, like a soccer player celebrating a goal an giving thanks. I touched the sand, and the coral shells, and saw Newstalk pull into the carpark: I rinsed in a dilapidated beach shower, and got changed, and we were out of there: on either side, snow-capped mountains; through the windscreen, snow coming down. And on my leg, blood: somehow, during the surf, I had opened up this wild scar tissue cut from Hawaii, and it didn't look that healthy – right on my shin, super sore.

But we were rushing: I knew I had held up the show, and he had to drop a board off in Cork, and it was snowing, and there were roadworks: the leg wasn't that big a priority. I mean, he wouldn't have let me die, but it wasn't a big thing: so it was totally bizarre, right then, emotionally. It was, for sure, a cocktail: there was stale adrenaline and images of epic waves; there was the sense that the trip to Ireland had a meaning. The board had worked, and the surf had been truly big: I was stoked; this was what I had been so, so, so hungry for, all that year in Hawaii I had strutted whatever skills I had; had hooked some challenging bombs; and knew, for sure, I was going to translate Irish skills to back Hawaii, as well, and represent, and show them that surfing those Irish waves was a whole other level – as well as the other way around.

(And here's another interesting thing: surfwear. Because – and you'll like me for this if you ever end up in–my shoes – there is a whole different sartorial dimension to the return trip than the way out. Outbound, you are looking for warmth – for protection, for survival: inbound, you are looking for something else: for shorts and t-shirts, or maybe just a towel, or anything else that will get you in the car faster: at that stage, you can't get any colder anyway. So I put my leg up on the dashboard, in my shorts, and just sort of reflected – in a quiet way, as we sped east – on the whole situation.

And the cocktail of reflection, no doubt, had some other ingredients, as I tried not to stare at my shin, and as we drove through Macroom: it had exhaustion, it had dehydration. It had a little grumpiness that Newstalk was sort of prioritising ding repair over my leg: it had exhaustion and regret and resentment at the paddle and the waves I had taken on the head and that gnarly, gnarly cliff descent. Had I really been ripping – or was I, as he put it, really just like someone called Wednesday Adams?

Was that the cocktail? Any way you sliced it, it was that same cigarette paper: that same super, super slim, hair's breadth, division between elation and despair.

But, yeah, it all worked out: sitting in the shaper's driveway, staring into space, the lads came and took a look at my leg. Next thing I know I am inside, in a warm friendly, chaotic Irish house, with his daughter just home from school and watching TV: next thing the shaper is cleaning it, and strapping it, and I am feeling like people are kind, people are good: feeling like surfers, though it seems like they hate each other, really don't, after all.

Ten out of Ten

Who says there is no poetry, no symmetry? Who says that things don't work out in this radical, celestial way: who says that chickens don't come home to roost, or that there are no second chances – who says you only live once?

At Kilcummin, at Castles, I was for sure living twice: a year down the track, and, literally, back on the muddy track to the shore: back across the country, and back through the same field (whose field was it, anyway?) – and standing, again, there among the briars and looking out, and seeing the same thing: the same slab, ledge, and set up. But feeling, for whatever reason, a little different: something in the air said that, maybe, this wasn't going to be that day: this wasn't, in whatever way – yet to b– defined – going to be the same thing as last year.

I was so, so stoked I had slept in: if we had been there earlier, I reckoned we would have gotten in at Castles on the low. But the tide had pushed, to Newstalk's total annoyance, leaving only one wave in town: back to Kilcummin, around the corner, and its long, long lefts outside the harbour mouth.

There were other layers to what was going on, as well: other moving parts, like Surfline. Surfline! What an institution: but Newstalk was old school, and scoffed at their forecasts; in fact, lets be honest, he hated them. They were impinging on his old school WAM model interpretations; they were often wrong; they didn't know –he spots – and they for sure didn't know the lesser-known spots.

But my heart was, for sure, in my mouth – as the old Irish expression goes. Killers was, is, forever will be, a challenging wave: not a fun place, not an easy place. A place of consequence, and a place where you can get drilled, and get in trouble, and don't want to be on your own: a place of extra, extra remoteness: Kilcummin is to Killala what Killala is to Ballina what Ballina is to Dublin what Dublin is to New York – that kind of thing. (Frog Rock is to Kilcummin what Killers is to Ballina, but that is another story).

But a place, as well – once we had checked, re-checked, gotten changed, and all of that – where you could, at least, get in: a place with steps down from the pier in to the ocean, landing you down in sheltered water – and a current that (bizarrely) didn't bring you in to the lineup, but away from it: a current that was benign, and friendly; a current that wasn't going to try and exhaust you to an inch of your life on your way back in.

And then, it was time: then it was showtime, and Foamo got a few, and Newstalk got a–few, and – you guessed it – I didn't get a few. I started missing waves. And not just missing the hard ones: three times, missed, on pretty easy – pretty–friendly – ones: miss, miss, miss. Leaning too far back, waves feeling too fast, too racy: too many moving parts; too little belief; the wrong technique. The third time, Newstalk looked back at me sort of balefully, as if to say, hey, you are wasting waves, please stop doing that: I chilled out, hung back, and considered, for a little while, just sulking the whole thing out.

I mean, it was a left: it was cold; I had hurt my toe in Kerry. It all wasn't aligning: my board was still dinged up, and the wetsuit still felt heavy, and it wasn't, on any level, coming together. My heart sank: it was déjà vu, it was the same thing, all over again, a year later.

And the waves, by the way – if it matters – were big: there were a few came through that Foamo, Newstalk and I just watched – ones that hit the reef further up, in some kinds of odd sloping way; just these huge sort of slopes of water – as if the reef was somehow rejecting them: they were breaking, but not in the normal way, and not in a way that invited any kind of surfing, that was for sure.

It was hypnotic, that kind of thinking: the only thing, maybe, that broke the spell was the distance. The miles travelled, the time, the everything, to get to this one point: it was a notching up of pressure: it was kill or cure, it was do or die, it was death or glory thinking. It was unwise, desperate, unhappy thinking: but at least it was thinking, and benign annoyance with myself, and the wheels, slowly, began to turn. Slowly, slowly, slowly: then faster and faster, as I got caught inside, and looked up, and saw Newstalk surfing past me on a good one, and knew – right then – that it was on.

And so I got out the back, and got one, and hung on with my toenails, and made the drop and the section and took the high line, and saw it mutate, and turn concave on the inside, right in front of me: and I got another, and another, and I started to wonder: what would it take? I mean, how many waves would justify it all? Some sessions, for some surfers, in some places, they just need one: but I wasn't like that, and so I asked myself: what about, maybe, ten waves? What about getting to ten? And not just ten, but what about ten good ones – would that be a runner? Would that, maybe, justify it all?

And so the count began, and I got to four, and five – but six more? That, for sure, still felt like a long way away. And then, right on cue, the lads went in: right on cue, I was out on my own, and the stakes felt a little higher, and it all felt a little mor– intense – and, you guessed it, the waves stopped coming. And the waves had been big, and were still big when they came, and were maybe bigger: certainly for sure, no exaggeration, my height – six-three – plus another one of me on top, easy. And there was a hiatus, and the whole thing hung in the balance – and then the waves started coming; and I was ok with being on my own; and the target was, for sure, more important than ever.

The target! That, maybe, was the absurd thing. Having the number to aim for, the numbers to keep track of: having the goal, the finish line; having the glittering prize, purely invented, purely imagined – having it to keep me company. Five, six, seven – and, woah, what was that? Was that the lads on the harbour wall; were there some hoots, and waves, and points in the right direction to paddle? Was that what was happening? Eight, nine – I think seven was a good one, but maybe it was eight – and were they some cameras in the lads' hands? And was I now, still, the only one out – apart from some German surfers who were way, way too far on the shoulder – was that what was happening? For reals?

That was the target, in my head: ten good ones. Was that high? Low? Artificial? But here, also, as well, is what else happened: here is how the green door really, really opened. The sun, ok, hadn't come out on a single surf trip so far – right? I mean, not at all: maybe for a moment at Easkey right, but that was it. And it was the same at Kilcummin, until it wasn't: It as the same low, leaden, cold grey skies – until it wasn't, and the clouds parted – right when I was at a hot streak in my ten for ten drive – and the sun, yes, came out.

But, this being magical, mystical Ireland, it didn't just come out: it illuminated. The land greenly glowed: it radiated. The cliffs from Kilcummin to Frog rock and down to castles turned green and gold: the cows looked happy, the land luminesced. It was, to be honest, emotionally overwhelming: it was a rush, numinous, it was mana, mana, mana. And, yes, I said thanks: redemption, resurrection, victory of the green. "Stay in Hawaii", Foamo had said to me earlier in the session, and he may have been right – but he may also have been wrong.

Maybe: yeah, maybe that was what was happening, as well. Eight, long pause, nine: long, long pause: ten. Ten, ten, ten: but why not eleven, right? I mean, why stop at ten, I said to myself, redrawing my–contract – breaking my own deal. But no – no, no, no: no dodging the silent pacts with the universe this time, buddy. Because, like magic – like a spell – after ten it was all over: the ocean shut down; the tide changed: the sun wen– in, the wind came up – the take-off spot moved down the point on the high tide; the Germans cursed it, and cursed their timing, and laughed, and smiled – and the waves closed out, and the tide killed it.

Was that it? Or was there one more thing? And how can I write this without – you know? Without..... I mean, how can I write that I paddled in, so easily – the crowning end to the session that turned it all around – that turned Ireland on its head – and came up the pier stairs, smooth as silk, water to land, and – on the empty pier, in the Irish winter, with no one around but us and the Germans – the lads clapped.

Maybe ironically, maybe just to stay warm – but they laughed, and clapped, as I walked up the pier. I mean, how can I write that in a cool, self-deprecating way -right? I mean, maybe I can't! Maybe there is no cool way of writing that: maybe it is true, maybe some things just shouldn't be written.

But it had been cold, and I had been on my own, and the pictures showed that the waves weren't small – and it had been one of those moments, and they don't happen often, and I laughed. And the churn of emotions, the back and forth, resurfaced: the mind-bending lines between Hawaii, an– Ireland – home–and away – were blurred again.

Hawaii 6: Just One More

Life is a beach.

El Nino

And.... Now.... Now what? What happens now, right? Back from Ireland, and things – somehow – seemed to plateau, open up, slow down, space out. Slow down, though, wasn't always good: no waves until, After two months – right at the end–of March – it seemed to awake. The feel was back – but would the dark side be as well? Probably, right? I had spoken with Doug earlier that day down by the beach. It is a golden spot, he had said: we need a printer, to print more copies of it – but trouble was never far away.

Was there such a thing as a bad year? "Once in a great while", said Greg, making it sound sort of mythical. But now it was happening, and things got edgy, for sure: I told Zach he was the colonel to my Elvis; he said he didn't like –y boards – that kind of thing. And it got a little too far out, at times, though more zany than anything else. I mean, did I really try to get back at Zach's latest umbrage by ordering a lot of squirrel stickers and decorating the stand where he parked–his bike – did that really happen?

It was so surfy, in a way so Spicoli – even though maybe, for someone who has been around the world a few times, for someone my age, sure: a little on the immature side, possibly. But, hey, you know what? That is surfing – if such a guru, such a sage, as Chuck could signal Mitch and get a pool noodle and soak unsuspecting tourists from behind the bathroom wall near the showers – attaching one end into the faucet and turning it into a hidden hose, Pump House Gang style – then yeah, I could stick up a few squirrel stickers as well. It would, maybe, have been rude not to.

The Beamish Boy

There is a breed of surfing hustler, that is for sure: the international chill merchant, blagging his way through. I never mastered it – possibly not cool enough or good enough: Christian Beamish – master shaper and board builder, and visiting from California – was on the other end of the scale super cool, and super good, and pretty much always welcome anywhere: equally far away from that vibe, right at the other end of the spectrum.

The big thing, though, was that there are people who turn up at different stages of life, and he was one of them. He had washed up on my shores, or vice versa, at pivotal times: when my Dad died, when I left San Francisco. When I split with a girlfriend: when I had originally left Ireland – and now – now. But why now? Why was I being forced to look in the mirror again? "Live your life in three-year increments", he said to me when I mentioned all this – and I was closing in on it, not having reckoned I would last even six months at the start.

So, suddenly – as well – I had that feeling of time passing: the rug-out-from under you feeling after a big night that the sun was now rising. Except now it was rising, like, three years later: how had it come to this? It had taken, for sure, the most bizarre constellation of events for it all to happen: how had someone who was not it to high rises – not into cities, not into crowds, and not really in to noise, and not super rich – lasted this long in twenty-first century Honolulu? Ans yet the constellation had happened: the low wise, low-fi surf shack on the Saratoga back street; the wave down the road; the three years at Three's.

Anyway! Christian didn't really have a mysto vibe, or anything, but the way he saw things, articulated things, could stop you in your tracks. Down at Kewalos, as we looked out at the surf, he just reached out his arms: "Man! Look at all that ocean. Now that, my friend, is an ocean". And it was: even to a Californian, the Pacific in Hawaii had this hugeness, this vastness to it. It just went on and on – Hawaii was just a dot in its realm – and, let's be honest, the swells barely noticed the place as they marched on through.

And he got me to thinking, as well: in Ireland, growing up, we had always called it the sea – something poetic, and that was sort of emotional, cerebral; something, via its monosyllabic name, that had a childish or even a primal resonance – something that you could, maybe, feel affection for, in terms of your whole connection with the element. But ocean? Ocean, *qua* ocean? The word conjured up such different things: was emblematic of the same spiritual vibe, for sure, but also of a hugeness, a power, that spoke – to me at least – of other gods.

His visit sort of spun me out in other ways, as well: I am a terrible host, it makes me edgy. I often try to get out of it, unlike my Mum and Dad – who hosted any blow-in, any time – which is probably, in fairness, what put me off it. But this time, when he opted for an extra night of big game hunting, Hemingway style, on the North Shore, I actually felt the absence: even in my surf shack, I would have preferred the guest.

When he came back, we surfed at you-know-where: in a bizarre moment that surfing could only throw up, as he sat on the board he looked like himself, but himself as a kid: wide eyed and stoked and messy hair; I got the weird feeling that I was, momentarily, taking to a stoked and interested twelve-year old mate.

Threes – he said to me emphatically – according to his mate from Sunset, wasn't just a good wave – it wasn't just the best wave on the south shore. It was, apparently, in a moment of wild expression, the best wave on the island. At first, I really didn't care what he, or his mate, thought: then, briefly, I did, and then I didn't again: who cares? Surfing isn't like that anymore; he would never see it at its best, anyway. I mean, I had been there three years – and Chuck said I had still only seen an eight?

The Slice

Let's face it: the time at Three's was a mere slice of it all. Not just a slice, but a slice of a slice of a slice: an infinitesimally small fraction of the waves of Hawaii, breaking all the way through the shoals of time. Maybe, if you really worked at it, you could run the numbers and work it out: let's say, you have, like, three regular crews at each spot, per day – yeah?

Then, let's say there are, maybe, a hundred spots that have stood the test of time – that have been surfed (let's say) for one hundred years. Or a–thousand – but, for now, let's say a hundred, in terms of the way surfing manifests itself in the modern era – let's leave it at that, just to simplify things.

So, doing some multiplication, that is a pretty high number – let's say it is a number like three hundred thousand, or something like that. And, out of all that, I had witnessed just one – been part of one crew, at one spot, for a couple of years. And that was it: was it, really anything to write home about? Well, maybe. Maybe, because maybe one wave is representative of all waves; maybe, in the same way that you can see every kind of wave in just one wave: maybe you can see every spot, every crew, every session, in one.

And sometimes, it could all happen in one day: paddle out from work, get some waves. Wind comes up, see a turtle. Get too many, or something, and face off with a wiry short boarder. A little chat on etiquette, camps formed, camps broken. Bonds forged and enmities lurking: Ralph paddles out, joins the fray: more waves, see Tom on the way in; show him the new concept shape. Meet Kavika and shoot the breeze: get to the showers, feeling like having lived all of Hawaii – and all of surfing – in around an hour.

Tom Crean's Ghost

Amazing things happen in threes: surfer, board, wave. Morning, noon night: tic, tac, toe. Three fins on your nice board, three turns on your wave: three wave sets and three o'clock surfs. And, of course, Threes, Threes, Threes. One thing, though, that was a little different – a little bit of an exception – was the three-man surf trip.

There was something about Kerry, as well, apparently. It had, to me, to do with Tom Crean: with the radical hardships he and Shackleton and the rest of the lads undertook in the Antarctic. The limited rations – the frostbite! The discomfort; tests of endurance; sickness: the cold. Having to kill seals and eat the dogs to survive: all of that kind of extreme, gnarly vibe. Kerry wasn't like that, but there was something about Crean, who came from that exact part of the country, in the air.

So when we pulled up at Inch and saw some waves coming through, I was sort of hanging back. And for once, yeah, it was a three-man mission, with a mate of Newstalk's on board as well (not a bad guy in any way), which also sort of shook me out of my comfort zone: triply on my guard, we went to check Annascaul, which was better – way better – but crowded.

Crowds! Such a scene. Some surfers love them, most hate them – but after the years in some of the busiest and most hectic lineups around, I really wasn't too bothered either way. I knew there would be maybe fifty percent of people not taking waves: half of them there just to be part of the scene. Of those who were taking the waves, well, no one could be on all the waves all the time – work on some dark arts, stay super alert, don't chat too much – all that, and – next thing you know – you have hooked a good one: and, if you don't get over excited, you are now legit.

So the crowd was no issue, but it was for others: outvoted by Newstalk and the Third Man, we tracked back to Inch. Still guarded, still thinking Crean, I took it easy as the lads legged it down the cliff (would Shackleton have been alarmed at the two speed, two group approach?): but the time I got to the bottom – perfect, imperfect timing – conditions had changed. Surfers were now retreating back up the cliff, or making for the beach, as what was almost a full-on storm – or at least a front – rolled through. Not having the climbing skills to get back up the cliff, I was, for sure, literally between a rock and a hard place – between the devil and the deep blue sea, baby.

As the weather worsened, and options narrowed – the tide was super low, so there was not, really, an option even to paddle out and then paddle to the beach – by this stage the whole reef was exposed, in all its slippery gnarliness – I was just over it. Finding a high-water rock and hoping the tide wouldn't nick my board,

I ditched it and scrambled back up. There, in the driving wind and rain, the only move seemed to be to drive the car down to the beach to see if I could intercept the lads on the sand. Last I had heard from another surfer they had headed in that way.

And so, in the wetsuit and in a strange car that kept cutting out at totally awkward times, and in the crazy sun and rain and wind and Irish summer warmth, and not even sure if I was doing the right thing, I tracked them down. Ok, cool: good move, everyone happy. And happy, as well, when Newstalk hooked a lift with another one of his mates to go and get my board back. And so me and the third man just sat in the carpark, and got changed, and shot the breeze. Just like in the Antarctic, things were veering back on to the realm of control of survival.

Not so fast, hombre: as we regrouped, and the lads thought about their morning calls, and – who knows – maybe regretting them a little, the only call seemed to be to get back to Annas again and brave the crowd. So that is what we did: back down the coast, back into the wetsuits, back into action.

But then there was the booties thing: this being a summer mission, I hadn't brought any. I mean, I didn't even have summer booties, anyway. So as the lads legged it ahead – again – I hung back and took the long way down in bare feet. For sure, I could have worn shoes, or something: but the whole trip was so far out by that stage, so surreal, that I was, to be honest, almost thinking of home. I was also, on anther level, sort of thinking how bad I would have done in the Antarctic: but there wasn't even time for that train of thought as I picked my way down the super stony track to the beach. I had to take the long way round because of the thorns on the shortcut: if we had gone in the morning we could have parked on the causeway, but that is a whole different story.

So things were getting rocky, getting bottomy, even before I reached the river mouth: even before I got though the crowd, and the surf-scenesters, and the slippy patches: but where was the rock bottom, really? Was it wading in to the river mouth and, in the midst of some kind of sulphuric grainy ooze, falling in headfirst? Was it when I got up and saw more rocks all the way to the lineup, and reckoned my feet just couldn't take it?

Maybe! Maybe it was then, or maybe it was later: wither way, walking back up to the car, defeated in every way – but at least vibing on a few Antarctic lessons – I had anew feeling, maybe something that had even been building up in Hawaii: I hated all things surfing. Hated the scenesters, the locals, all looking so happy or so serious: hated, just then the whole vibe.

The only solace, strangely, was from some non-surfer local jack the lads. "How are ye", they said, heads miles out the window, as they sped to a halt – maybe sensing my distress. "Any parking down there?" Four lads in a car, packed in there: pale and pudgy and sort of malign; smoke and chancer energy oozing from the windows. These lads were not surfers on any level – they were anti-surfers: but, at that moment, I loved them for it. Loved them for the way they didn't care about waves, or surfers, or surfing: loved the way they said they would park where they wanted, boy, without caring if they stepped on any sensitive surfer toes.

They were still in my head when the lads came back up, maybe an hour later: still in my head when the lads raved about their waves, and still in my head when, inspired by the chancers, I lit a cigar as we were putting on the roof racks. A smoking surfer! A shock to the purity, the health, the physical fitness vibe. But there was still a five-hour drive home to deal with, and I wasn't sure how I was going to manage it: but at least I was at home, and at least the jet lag kicked in again, and at least I didn't have to talk – or listen, or anything – and I woke up in Dublin.

The Shadow Line

I wondered, often, if the universe wanted me to stay in Hawaii forever. And I thought about what Hawaii had given me: the recovery from injuries, the health, the surfing style. And I thought about the rest of the world, places like Italy: and I thought about life post-surfing, and the older guys just hanging on to it. "We are all out here because we have a habit", said Lyndsay as he paddled up to me one day.

Looking at the old schoolers in that sort of light also helped to put the focus on the wave into perspective: looked at in one light, they could be looked at as some kind of ultimate. "Be careful", another old beach boy told me. "They are a cautionary tale, those guys at Threes; they are a terrible warning, as well as a good example. They are the ones who the spell cast such a strong effect over that everything else faded away: they are the devotees – they are part of the reef and the ocean out there. They took the blue pill, drank the Kool Aid, stayed in Tír na nÓg, and will have their ashes spread there one day: they listened to the siren song. They are the oceanic monks: they are the ones who find higher powers out there, like they find them nowhere else. They live the best life – and they are the lucky ones, the survivors – but it is not the only life."

And it was the best: the place, I can tell you, honestly, was enchanted. Not just that during those sunsets I experienced every conceivable emotion – from tears of joy to tears of distress; from boredom to elation to despondency to stoke to pain to an unreal lightness of being, bodily and mentally. On bad days, the place, seriously, could console you: could send a wave your way to make you feel better. If you were too high, it could ignore you: dismiss you, starve you.

Even over at Pops, which I was learning could be super hollow on the right swell direction (could be even a better wave that the hallowed ones, if you gave it a chance) I could totally trip out. The sun in the curl as the wave walled up: the speed, the glistningness of it all – and boom, you are on the treadmill, baby. You are paddling back out, and looking for another one – a better one, or even a lesser one: you are out there until dark! By which time you have, in some kind of way, sucked the absolute essence – as much as you possibly, humanly, can – out of the situation.

But what also blew my mind, talking to Barry, owner of the old school Inter-Island Surf Shop, was the lack of impact the wave – the place– surfing – could make. After all those years, I asked him his best wave story: he sort of looked in to space: it wasn't coming through as a picture or a narrative, even though you could just tell that as there.

And yikes, yikes, yikes: what was this? A new twist? Another turn? What was happening? I mean, sure: Ireland had tried to kill me, but by now I knew Hawaii had teeth as well. There were signs of changes of metaphorical seasons new challenges: tricky parts were threatening to outweigh curative elements. The Pagoda was under pressure to sell up (I realised now I would never, ever, ever have had such a killer place, killer time, killer experience without the pandemic – or without Alden and Chris, who had let me stay on way, way, longer than anyone else): my injuries were getting sore; work was banning telework – el Nino was on the way. And was I getting tourist fever – resort fever? Was I taking the long, long holiday for granted – was I getting too much, where most people just got a slice? Who was I, anyway? "How is the water?" asked an old school Hawaiian – who maybe had felt to same way for a lot longer than I had – as he cycled past me, coming back from the beach: "Enjoy it – it is the only thing we have left that is free."

And what else was happening? As I sat in Kelly's, I wondered, sometimes, about that. My body was booming – my posture had gotten so good that Zach asked me what was with the Zoolander thing; everyone got a little more of the Adonis vibe from Hawaii, even me – but other things were also happening: my eyes were getting fried from too much sun, my sinuses were a mess. I had some kind of overuse injury in my shoulder: despite the youthfulness of Hawaii, I wasn't getting younger: at one point, near the end of the third year, I had a sore knee from Coco Head, a dinged up wrist that just wasn't getting better, and a big cut on my heel from Kewalos – plus a sore groin from the board, and a sore shoulder and neck from sleeping in crazy positions.

A sore throat; and a giant bee sting on my arm, a jelly fish thing on my chest – for sure, probably I would have picked up some dings had I stayed in Ireland or California, but was this really all that healthy? I was – to be totally honest – getting older, and Threes would regularly remind me of it: so much of life now rotated around being ready for when the swell came up. Swimming, runs, work, people – times to eat and sleep and travel: they all had to pivot around being in the right place at the right time, out there in the Pacific.

I feared change: but maybe it was good – maybe, in a good way, the bubble needed to be burst. The four things I guess I had in mind when I came to Hawaii – surf; having a really good time; health; and work – had switched out in order from time to time, but waves and fun in the sun had, for better or for worse, almost always come first. The journey with Kimo, as well, had gone totally wild: by now I was on a seven-one double-ender step (and 'S') deck with a Brewer beak and quad option – and more width and thickness than I had ever seen: somehow, things seemed to be reaching the outer limits.

Reality, baby, was closing in: sitting in Arnold's one night, a Kauai fireman, out for his captain's retirement, told me that although his house was now super expensive, there was no way his kids were going to be able afford to live in Hawaii. And so – yeah, again – was that actually what was happening? Was life turning into some kind of Tom Petty song, when one moment it is all at your feet and the next moment you are on your knees? Was that the vibe? Or was it a Count of Monte Cristo thing, trapped by what sustained you – could too much of a good thing really be bad? Were things – sort of – accumulating? Should you quit when you were ahead – or at least not too far behind? Could you be like Eric Cantona – the football player who walked away from it all at the very peak of his game? Could anyone really have that strength? Mitch was getting ready to leave the locale become a lifeguard; Skipper Dave had moved to China. I mean, even James Bond had died!

I had listened to an older surfer, Wayne Lynch, say in a surf move that if he hadn't learned and done enough from the frost million waves, was it really going to happen in the second million: in the same way, maybe, one time – even though, yeah, I was feeling edgy from taking antibiotics – I found myself way over at

Paradise, looking at the crowd at Threes, and just feeling totally indifferent.

Time was passing, I guess: Hawaii is a fabulous place, a healing place: it was, is, will be. Good for the soul, the mind, the body – if you play your cards right. If not, though, it can take a toll, as well: Hawaii is, for sure, a place of violent natural extremes. Quiet, until it isn't: peaceful, until hurricanes or volcanic eruptions or wildfires strike. Jagged lava rock beneath the green mountain tops – big bad fish beneath the blue waters. Searing UV that would fry your skin and your eyes behind the gentle sun rays: the waves, the culture, the people, the vibe, all prone – just like in Ireland – to some form of extremism.

And, yeah, maybe that was what people sought on Hawaii, anyway: maybe in its master blaster style, Hawaii would sort of get everything out of your system, with bells on, if you gave it the time – gave it the chance. Waves – so many that I would almost feel like I was surfing when I was walking, some days – beach, rest, reflection, sun, aquamarine – almost to excess. I mean, you could even almost say that addictions – those gnarly things, those unconquerable things – could been vanquished by its very extremes. And was it done with me now – would the hunger for it all ever return?

Even Gerry Lopez – everyone knows who Gerry Lopez is, right? – even he had left; even he had concluded, on some level, that too much of a good thing could be bad. But maybe it wasn't even that: maybe it was the brightness, the hotness; the swelteringness of it all: maybe it was the trade winds and the kona winds, and the occasional hurricane, and the way that – even if you had it all of that dialled in – it could just erode you, somehow.

But – now that I am on a roll – what else was happening? Where had all this new time and space and spare capacity come from? Was it Hawaii – was that what it was? Had Hawaii, and Covid, and all the rest, given me a chance to sort out all the kinks, all the dings – physically, behaviourally, even spiritually – and make me, perish the thought, almost normal? Regular – capable? Was that it? And, likewise, was there that edge, that fatal edge, to do with the sheer beautiful, pointlessness of surfing – but, fundamentally, pointlessness – creeping in? Was that why I could now come in from killer, killer waves and feel like I had, maybe, just had a glass of wine – rather than ten whiskeys?

Who knows: maybe some kind of awareness of the wider world was creeping back in – which may not, to be totally honest, have been a bad thing. Would all the glee have been there without the background cast – the pit teams; the enablers; the distant supporters? Was I going to wake up one day and realise I couldn't have done it without them, and that I now no longer could?

I mean, picture a bus, right? Picture a public bus – something in the public domain. Then picture buses of different sizes, but each with only one seat: then, if you can – if you feel like it – picture the line at the bus stop, and picture people barging to the front of the line when the nice, big bus comes by. Then, just to add the golden, finishing touches – picture the bus ride. Picture the way the bus just goes around the block, and then drops you off, and then you have to walk back to the bus stop: sometimes, for better or for worse, that is the way surfing could feel; that, honestly was how absurd surfing felt like it could be.

"Hawaii is amazing, right up until it isn't", I heard a military guy say in the pub one night. I didn't agree, but I mean – what I am saying is – had the place worked its magic? And, if so – what happened next? Every quasi-hippy retreat had its parabola, right? Had its bell curve: its sweet spot, before it played itself out? Did the plasticky side of Waikiki start to overwhelm, and tell you it was time to hit the road? Was it the anonymity amongst so much company: the constant churn of humanity – would I start to feel the boundaries of my square mile more and more? Was the journey from fried, to burned out, to played out, through to Hawaiian healing – the *reclusion*; the whole Papillon vibe – nearly complete?

Even the vibe in the ocean had changed: but, yeah, even now, there could still be transcendent moments, like the evening Pete and I sat out there with some wild vortex cloud overhead and caught these effortless, flowing little runners as the sun set – the ocean truly felt heling on those evenings, like it was literally trying to fix your body. Or the time, for whatever reason, when it was just me and Chuck and Dave and Zach, one Sunday evening, and the waves just fired – and it was just this joy not to have to fight for them, as if I were in Ireland.

But there was a repetitiveness starting, despite every effort to push it back, to creep in. So, yeah, it was sort of a battle. Darren – the Kiwi helicopter pilot who lived in his van and surfed pretty hard, would philosophise over it in the Ala Moana sun. He was a good surfer, but was sceptical of the glitz of surfing in Hawaii – the local and international media machine that drove the image, if not the reality – and that could often deceive. He was sceptical of the crowds, the localism, even the quality of the waves. "It's actually not that great", he would say; sometimes, I would agree. Ireland, I had learned, had more and better waves – even than the North Shore.

Back at the Cole memorial, there had been a moment, as well: one of those moments that seem sort of innocuous, but that I kept tracking back to: a former super surfer, super model, golden balls, *ubermensch* – sitting there, looking ok, but with his wrist in a cast. And suddenly he just looked like an older man who was injured: not what you want to see, right? And yet all surfing roads lead there – unless you can somehow find the strength to take the Cantona approach.

And I was also – if it's not too deep, not too existential – continually crossing and re-crossing all these shadow lines – not just between youth and age, but between being away and being home. Sometimes, maybe, it got sort of tiring. But – not to get profound, or anything – what about this: what about the idea that you never know how far below your limit you were – five percent, fifty percent – until you have hit your limit? What about the idea that each new stage of life is a product of the last? What about the end not really being evident – it being just a feeling, an instinct – until it happens? What about the question in the song that asks if it all ended tomorrow – would you be ok with that? Could you adjust to the fall?

And, speaking of Hawaii, and speaking of Ireland – what was the connection there, anyway? Ireland always had this sort of crucible vibe – a place of births and beginnings, and getting out to colonise, informally, through pubs and graft and whatever else. A place of beginnings – so was Hawaii a place of endings? Was the place another end point in a cycle – would it have to start again somewhere else, somehow?

It had been a trip, that was for sure: dinner times determined by sunset; waves lapping on the beach in a state of dreaminess. The gekkos, eyeballing me as I used the garden hose to rinse off every day. The simplicity was maybe the most intoxicating part – but it was all, sort of, ephemeral: a sunset was amazing, for sure, but it only lasted pretty much exactly as long as a sunset lasts.

Yet even then, for sure – again – flashes of the pure, intoxicating, sublime transcendence of the place would return, and blindside: days when, glassy and overcast, waves would come through amidst stoked faces that would just sort of wipe everything out: that would reset you, and take you to another dimension, and from deep within the bubble make all thoughts of departure laughable. Even though I couldn't always track all of the different vibes –was Chuck upset with me now? Was Daniel now shouting me into waves, saying "Go Sea Bass"? – there were days when the spell would be cast anew, and you would feel like going out all night afterwards. Maybe the spell had loosened its grip – but all it needed was a twitch on the thread.

The Days in Between

So, what was it all about, in the end? I mean, what, basically, was the point? Was it, maybe, one of those ironies – one of those kind of things where you can't see the wood for the trees, or something like that? Was it – as in, surfing at Three's – actually, nothing at all to do with any of the big events – the memories – but something, maybe, to do with the spaces in between: about the moments that don't make the stories? Was that it?

Maybe, yeah. Maybe that was it. Maybe – and not to romanticise it, or anything – it was about the small days, the off days: the days when the reports didn't hype it up. The days when it was quiet, sort of, and when maybe just Glen or Jon or Greg or Chuck or whoever was out. And, at some point in the evening – yes, for sure, you might get a nod to look in a certain direction. A suggestion, a tilt of the head, to look at the radical pink light at Diamond Head, or the shouldering sunset on the other side, or some kind of rainbow, or mountain view, or cloud formation, or whatever. A glassiness in the water, or the colour of the water, or a turtle passing by – just a raised eyebrow; a recognition.

And, as all that happened, one by one, the lights of Honolulu would come on, and you would check your position against the lineup markers again, and check the sights, and catch another runner, and watch the sun set, and see the light change. And the tourist boats would roll by, with their last batch of drunken revellers, singing and hooting – and you got that feeling of living in a touristy place, where every visitor felt like they were an individual, having the most unique drunken tropical maritime high – but, sometimes, it just felt like the latest batch. Take a number, broski: you felt the arrogance and the privilege and the protectiveness of the local, maybe, as the sun set at Three's.

And of course it wasn't all about that – no way: there were sublime pau hana Friday nights, and hikes with mates from work through the verdant, intense, dark volcano-jungle trails above town. And there were the birds, and the turtles who would surface right beside you, and who you could just chill with for as long as you needed when you were snorkelling. And there was the supreme diversity of Hawaii, with all its different races and creeds and nationalities and histories, that both mattered and didn't matter at all. And there was mythology: there was the way Kamaka, the doorman at Kelly's, would tell me radical stores of night marchers and menehune. (The parallels between Hawaii and Eire sometimes totally blew my mind. The leprechauns and the menehune; the island karma; the touristy-ness: the same sort of sincere, tokenistic use of old languages.)

So no way was it all about Threes: there was the North Shore, with all its power and its glory – and there were all the reasons not to go there, from parking to traffic to locals to crowds to vibes to danger, danger, danger – to the drive, to the way the waves were – sorry – sort of similar to the West of Ireland. And there were the other waves: at Pokai Bay, on the West Side. At Hickham and Malekahana and the Rest Camp and wherever else: there were walks to Diamond Head to watch Cliffs and Lighthouse breaking.

And there was a lot, lot else: wild nights seeing Zach's band play, and his tortilla nights when it would be just surf talk all the way. And there was the way the maintenance guy, Alden, would give me fish, and there was the Thanksgiving Day with Kimo when – no joke – he ate, and slept, and watched football, and then shaped a board for me.

And there was Masao the fisherman, always telling me what time the fireworks were on at – because he wasn't just fisherman, but also a pyrotechnician: and there was working life, across the road on Fort de Russey: and there were beach clean-ups with Surfrider, where you could get thorns that went all the way through your flip-flop.

And there were the scary, scary centipedes, and there was the way that it always rained on Saturday nights: and it did, for whatever bizarre reason, It would pour, for a little while, each Saturday. What was it? Was it something, maybe, to do with all the people pouring into Waikiki, changing the micro climate? Was it a message from the gods, saying to cool it – don't get too crazy? Who knew, but I can testify to it: another element of mystique of Hawaiian life.

And there were the other details, as well: the walks back from the beach with Masao and Zach. The conversations – on, say, scorpion fish – on the grass verge, in the dark: no one really in a rush, everyone vibing from the ocean. On those occasions, the squirrel shish kebab motif, which had become totally enduring, would surface again, unannounced: Masao would go off on a riff about squirrel-style personal habits; Mitch would double over with laughter whenever the word was mentioned. I mean, to call someone a squirrel – it seemed like there could be nothing worse, in the alternate universe we were living in. It was a term of endearment as well as pejorative, though, which was cool as well.

But, yeah, to be totally honest, it maybe actually was all about that sunset at Three's, on those days in between: Around then, Zach would usually paddle out, commenting on Russia and Ukraine, or politics, or the latest news, or whatever. Not always ideal, but who cared: there was, in essence, a pattern: a simplicity, and a chill vibe that formed the tapestry of the days that no one remembered; the days it was all about; the fabric of the time and the place: the days in between.

Who Knows

So, at the end of the day, Hawaii could do a few different things to you: it could chew you up and spit you out; it could embrace you and never let you leave. It could traumatise, shock, bore, fascinate: it could make you feel at the centre of the universe, or the edge of the world. I knew I was too far from Ireland, but had stayed longer than I thought I could have: knew that, like a lot of things, a lot of places, Hawaii was easy to leave, right up until it wasn't – that you could say goodbye, mahalo – just like with Ireland – right up until she was, as the song goes, walking out the door. But then you get on the plane, and somewhere along the way, perspectives change: the world opens out again, and the autodidact vibe, the local hero energy, and the whole scale of the thing, sort of fades.

Zach and I had gone out to a vegan sushi place – yes, roger that – and we had talked about the Threes journey. It had been, pretty much, two years since I first really got to grips with the place – and it sort of seemed like it was being marked. There was a slap on the shoulder, a pat on the back, before we went on to see aging reggae guru Pato Banton – that night, there was a little bit of a vibe that said – without saying it – "Hey, you have done ok in these Hawaiian waves". Hey, if anyone had the right to judge, it was him: it was only now dawning on me the tireless, relentless work – for whatever reasons – Zach had put into my health, my surfing, my approach to life, over the last three years. It went way, way beyond technique: way more to do with the way that surfing was so social – like, ninety percent – and that if you were both cool and capable that was the only way you would be ok, and maybe not even then.

I mean, he had been tireless: every day – pretty much every single day there was surf, which was all lot of days – for weeks and months – and now years – on end. Technique, balance, yoga, spiritualism, religion, lifestyle, diet: the environment, books, holistic therapies, the history and future of the world, the turtles, the sharks. He had turned me, maybe, into some kind of island-style ubermensch, but only by pouring himself into the effort: only by relentlessly, over and over, drilling in the lessons. "You never listen", he said.

But other things happened, as well: the cycle of surfing, I was learning, never ends: old schoolers were retiring, new lads coming on the scene. Chris, a lad from Texas, was getting to grips with the ocean. He was good natured and was, in some ways, the new apprentice: I was, for better or for worse, no longer the new guy. It wasn't so much, with all this going on, about crossing the bridge when I come to it, but to, actually, crossing the bridge once I am over it – you know?

And yet there were flip sides to the flip sides: the transcendence, the super stoke, could hit hard, and suddenly, like a wave itself: sitting with the fishermen at Kewalos at the end of my run, the mellowness – the sun, the shade, the trees, the watch-the-world-pass sort of vibe – was just the best, *the crème de la crème*. One of those situations where something would happen – someone having a few too many beers, or someone walking by with a fish, or a net, or a dog, or whatever – and that would be it: fuel for discussion for a couple of hours, easy.

Life had swung, that was for sure: through a fishing mate in Ireland who sold antiques to wealthy people, I had had an intro, when I arrived in Hawaii, to a posh place in Diamond Head – the eastern end of my spectrum. That was where it began, in some kind of way: now, towards what was maybe the end, I was with the fishermen in Kewalos – the other end of the spectrum, geographically and socially. These guys were not rich, that was for sure: but they did hard jobs: worked in freezers, chefs, drove delivery vans. A paramedic, maybe.

That was, for whatever reason, how it had shaken out: but you learned things, cool things, from the fishermen. Small things, details: the way that Hawaii traffic had not been so bad ten years ago, but was now spiralling out of control: the way that if you just had a fishing pole up the HPD would sometimes let you get away with dodging some parking rules. Small things, cool things.

And maybe, possibly, that was – when I tried to work it out – what it was all about: maybe that was it. Maybe there are events in life – sensations, places, people, whatever – that, like with Barry. don't actually get remembered. That just happen, and are gone, like a wave – so, really – I mean really – did any of this even happen? Zach? Chuck? The waves – Hawaii? For sure, it did: but for those parts that didn't stick in my mind, that didn't get memorialised? Well, I salute them as well. Because maybe we all need times of life when receptors and analytical tools and narratives are switched off: maybe it is good, maybe it is healthy. Times when, to be honest, nothing really happens – and not in a bad way – in between the times when they do: And maybe, possibly, that is what sunset at Three's, ironically, was all about.

And, whether I was staying or going, at least things had settled: I was part of the furniture. "Is it five-thirty", Chuck asked, one day, and just by indicating that the line up was cool with me: Zach would go into deep metaphysical ramblings about religion versus spirituality in between sets late in the day. One night, an SUP guy was out. He had been, he told me, a former North Shore surfer until he hurt his back. I was riding one in as he was coming back out: "I just loved watching you on that wave, he said: "You rode the pocket the whole way through". I laughed with stoke: that, maybe, was what it all boiled down to: for an Irishman to hear those words in Hawaii. Whatever the future held, at least I had done something – even if it was only that.

And Thanks!

The Kewalos fishermen

"That was so beautiful", said, Christina during a big swell – though I am pretty sure she was talking about the wave, not the way I had surfed it. But, you never know.... "You got some fun ones", said Dustin after the big swell. "You got a lot of nice waves", said the surfer on the inside, one day. "That was beautiful", said a lady I was surfing with at Paradise: "I love watching him surf", said a guy who had been coming out a lot, and who had been talking to the lady. (Was he just being nice to try to chat her up?). "That was a hero wave", said Kyle one day; "That was so beautiful", said Chris after a big swell bomber – "You read the wave so well", said Jon one day.

"You get all the good ones", said an unnamed surfer – "you make it look so easy", said an Asian lady; "You're having a good session", said the people at Paradise: "And you", said Ralph; "you got some as well", when we discussed the swell from the year before on the roadside with Tom, and who got what. "I was a tiny bit jealous of your waves", said Kyle, again, as a day when he was at Three's but should have been with me at Paradise: 'You got some speed on that machine", said the Hawaiian tattooed muscleman.

"You lucky bastard – do you want a beer?" said the catamaran driver as the cruised past and watched me surf some waves, on my own, on a Saturday night, in the oily sunset deep blue and gold waters. "You got a sick one, but the one after that was even sicker," said Noah, the longboarder on a night when the waves – deep, deep blue – were tinged and tinted with glowing glitter orange from the sunset.

Yeah – I know, I know. But, hold up: what if, maybe, I have focused a little too much on the hard-knocks side of surfing in Hawaii? What if I have forgotten those kind of words, those kind of comments – that, each one, when said, feels, honestly, like a medal: each one an award, and something that you sort of hold on to. As Oscar Wilde once said, "I can live off a complement for two weeks" – and that is pretty much the case.

"Nice waves today, *cabron*", said Zach, cycling off into the night. So thanks, thanks, thanks. Because, at the end of the day, maybe it was meant, or not – maybe it was just being polite. But those things don't come easy, especially in Hawaii, and they are, at the end of the day, the barometer of progress. So thanks – mahalo: you all surfed nice too.

Epilogue: The Greatest

A long time before all this happened, in Ireland, this killer pod of dolphins had moved into the local beach: they just sort of hung out for a while, maybe a few months, and then moved on. There was attention, there was hype: there were people coming to the beach from all over, just to see them. And there was this one, major, unreal experience that I had: there was this one day when I swam, like usual, out to the marker buoy – less than a mile from where I had grown up, and pretty much spent a lot of my life.

Swim out, chill, swim back: that was the groove, summer pace, home pace. Usually, that was the vibe – but not today. Not this time: this time, the dolphins appeared, maybe four or five of them, and – no joke – began to circle me in a pretty surreal, unreal, sublime way: circling maybe like five meters away, just languidly: circling, spaced out evenly like in some kind of show; surfacing and rolling on their backs, and sort of eyeballing me.

That whole thing went on for a while: went on maybe for five or ten minutes, and then they just faded out, and I swam in, tripping out. And – going up the steps home – this local lady, an old lady, Pat Burke, stopped me and said she had seen the whole thing. And she had this sort of mystical look, as if to say that it had been a big deal for her: and it had been, for me as well. It was, for sure and to this day, the greatest thing that had ever happened to me in the ocean.

And that is the kicker – that is the ringer, that is the whole point: that Hawaii was, is, and I guess will probably always be a land of absolutes: a land of absolute sun, beach, surf, ocean. Always the archetype, always the model: and Ireland, on those levels – and, maybe, on every level – is the opposite: a place or relativism, where a sunny day escalates in value in the context of the rain and the cold and the clouds: a place where things like being circled by a pod of visiting dolphins just never happens – until, one day, it does.

Paintings by Elizabeth Cope

(featured on the cover of this book)

2023

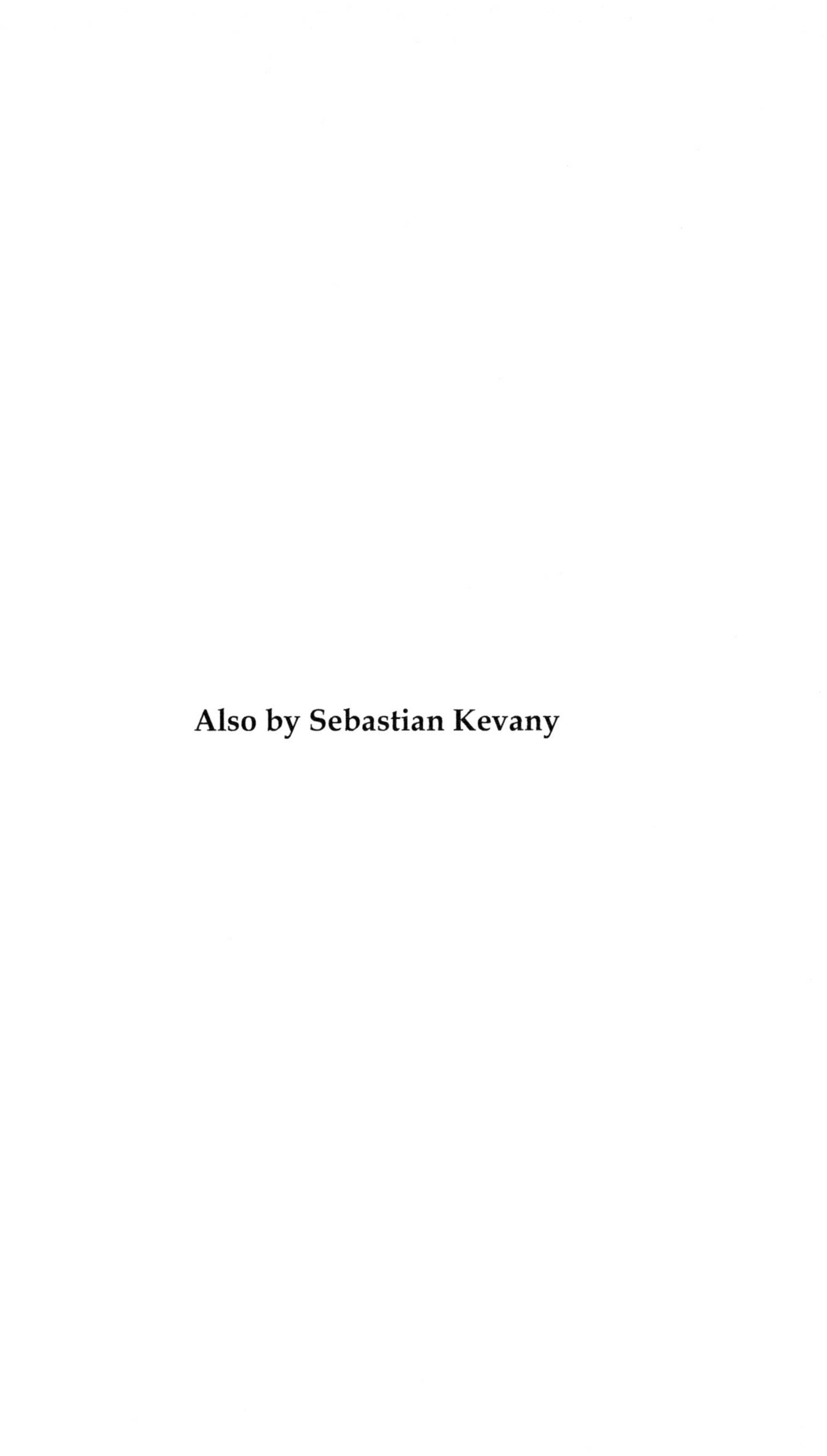

Also by Sebastian Kevany

What They Said About

Between the Moon and the Fire: Life in Surfing Moments
by **Sebastian 'Bassie' Kevany**

"A sun-drenched, blue-tinted collage of surfing snapshots" – **Andy Martin**

"The well-travelled Sebastian Kevany has surfed around the world many times at plenty of well and lesser-known places. He is a very observant man who has enjoyed numerous close interactions with various people and cultures. This memoir is filled with thoughtful insights from his experiences and adventures along the international surfer's trail. Lots to dip into and enjoy for all thinking surfers who like to read." – **Wayne Murphy**

"Surfing is about more than riding waves. Sebastian Kevany clearly gets that. Read this book to find out why…" – **Scott Laderman**

"Sebastian captures the long-standing spirit of Irish surfing, and updates my own experiences of surfaris, adventure, and fun." – **Kevin Cavey**

"This book depicts many sublime moments of adventure, exploration and surfing from the intuitive mind of the gifted surf traveller and academic that is Sebastian Kevany. … A true breath of fresh sea air in the ever-evolving culture of surf! Míle buíochas (a thousand thanks)!" – **Dr. Eoin McCarthy Deering**

Available to buy online in print and e-book editions. For further information, please visit:

www.TMPpublications.com

Fever in the Jungle: Inside the World of an Epidemic Troubleshooter

What is life really like amidst the global battle against epidemics and infectious diseases? In *Fever in the Jungle*, Sebastian Kevany draws on his experiences of over more than one hundred treatment, prevention and outbreak missions, in some of the most remote corners of the world. Amidst the fight against HIV/AIDS, tuberculosis, malaria and Ebola, he takes us out of hotel room bubbles and, not just off the beaten track – but to the places where there are no tracks at all.

Fever in the Jungle describes, in vivid detail, the successes and defeats of a field epidemiologist, troubleshooter, liaison, barefoot diplomat and jack-of-all-trades. From rattling convoys and ramshackle malaria clinics in South Sudan, to air-conditioned meetings with government officials in Sierra Leone – with a few full-moon parties along the way – this is a window into the often bizarre challenges, places and adventures that make up an occasionally chaotic, often unpredictable yet, always fulfilling existence.

What They Said About

Fever in the Jungle: Inside the World of an Epidemic Troubleshooter by **Sebastian 'Bassie' Kevany**

"This splendid book reminds me of my own experiences, travelling in various places of the world more than sixty years ago. Hopefully, as is suggested herein, things are changing. I wish Bassie the best of fortune in the splendid work he does." – **Peter Somerville-Large**

"Sebastian captures the fine line between success and failure in tackling some of the greatest challenges facing humanity… a book that will inspire involvement in the work of epidemic control in inhospitable places." – **Mark Pollock**

"Fever in the Jungle *is one-part epidemiological field guide, and one-part adventure novel. This book offers a unique insight into the on-the-ground practices and dangers of global disease prevention and control. A must-read for those who like to be informed while entertained."* – **Professor Garrett Wallace Brown**

"We are transported to places where reality surpasses imagination, leaving the reader with a sense of participation in the world's epochal challenges." – **Dr. Michel Rubbini**

"Sebastian has gained immesurable field experience through his participation in various epidemic, health emergency, and humanitarian crisis responses – especially in the developing world. I strongly recommend everyone to explore his journeys!" – **Dr. Vijay Kumar Chattu**

Available to buy online in print and e-book editions. For further information, please visit:

www.TMPpublications.com

Printed in Great Britain
by Amazon